BEYOND THE AMERICAN DREAM

A Family's Unscripted Journey Abroad

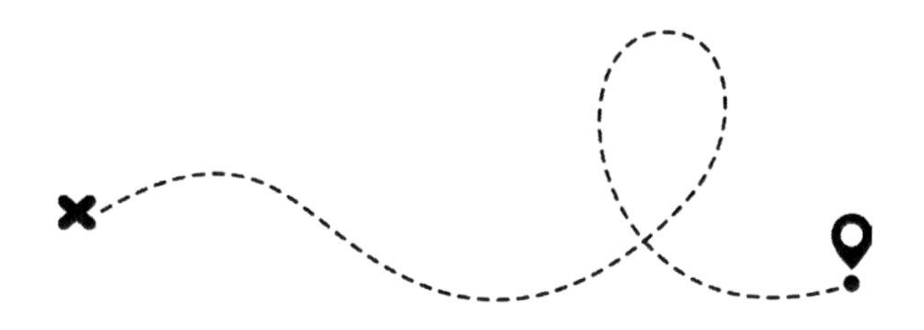

JAMES ROXAS BALAGOT

For Maricar and our children,
Jero, Lea, and Feris.

Thanks for making every day an adventure.

CONTENTS

AUTHOR'S NOTE 1

PROLOGUE: **PROMISE ME** 2
Jakarta, October 2006

PART ONE
REDEFINING OUR PATH

1 **IS THIS SOMETHING YOU WILL REGRET?** 15
November 2013

2 **LIFE ON TRACK** 21
May 2014

3 **WHAT IS YOUR DREAM VACATION?** 29
August 2017

4 **OUR TIPPING POINT** 36
November 2018

5 **WE JUST NEED ONE YES** 47
January 2019

6 **WHEN DO WE GO PUBLIC?** 60
February 2019

7 **BOX, SELL, OR DONATE** 66
May 2019

8 **CAN I CHANGE MY ANSWER?** 79
July 2019

PART TWO
OUR JOURNEY UNSCRIPTED

9 **GOT A EURO?** 85
Berlin, July 2019 (Week 0)

10 **TRAIN TO PRAGUE** 97
Prague, September 2019 (Week 6)

11 **WE HAVE NOTHING TO WORRY ABOUT** 107
Napoli, February 2020 (Week 27)

12 **THE ONE-ROOM SCHOOL HOUSE** 124
Berlin, April 2020 (Week 36)

13 **MICROADVENTURING IN OUR BACKYARD** 143
Berlin, April 2020 (Week 36)

14 **COULD WE DO THIS FOREVER?** 149
Croatia & France, July 2020 (Week 53)

15 **TRAVELING ON BORROWED TIME** 173
Greece, October 2020 (Week 66)

16 **COVID IS BACK, AND IT'S DARKER** 193
Berlin, November 2020 (Week 70)

17 **THIS CAN'T BE THE END** 203
Berlin, November 2020 (Week 72)

18 **WE PROBABLY SHOULDN'T, BUT WE DID** 219
Rome, December 2020 (Week 74)

19 **PLAYING BY THE RULES** 231
Berlin, February 2021 (Week 83)

20 **HARDLY SURVIVING THE LAND OF FIRE AND ICE** ... 236
Iceland, April 2021 (Week 91)

21 **THIS TIME, IT'S NOT MY FAULT** 253
Mallorca, June 2021 (Week 97)

22 **SATISFIED?** 264
Switzerland, June 2021 (Week 98)

23 **SQUEEZING IN IMPOSSIBLE** 271
Turkey, July 2021 (Week 100)

24 **DOES EVERYONE KNOW SOMETHING WE DON'T?** 279
Istanbul, July 2021 (Week 102)

25 **LOCKED DOWN FOR 21 DAYS** 292
Hong Kong, July 2021 (Week 103)

26 **OFFICIALLY DAY ONE** 308
Hong Kong, August 2021 (Week 105)

27 **REMEMBER, YOU SIGNED UP FOR THIS** 318
Hong Kong, March 2022 (Week 137)

EPILOGUE 327
San Francisco, July 2022

Q&A WITH JERO, LEA, AND FERIS 330

AUTHOR'S NOTE

This adventure memoir started as a personal weekly letter to my children as a way to capture our journey and experiences. It has also served as an immediate reminder of why we chose our path and seek more.

As our journey continues, I have realized that others may question their path to happiness and success. For those who think there is only one correct path and who ask, "What if?" I encourage you to explore your desires, pursue the possibilities, and make opportunities happen. I hope our story proves that you don't need all the answers, are capable of weathering challenges (both small and global), and can find adventure anytime, anywhere.

Finally, it was important that Maricar and I listened to our kids and what they wanted out of this journey as well. As parents, it has been a delightful privilege to expose them to many beautiful places and cultural experiences while learning alongside them. Throughout the book, Jero, Lea, and Feris will share their unfiltered opinions in sections entitled "In Their Words." Furthermore, there is a Q&A at the end of the book where they share their favorite memories, frustrations, and thoughts on the past five years.

—James

PROLOGUE

PROMISE ME

Jakarta, October 2006

Maricar and I met at the University of California Los Angeles (UCLA) in 2000 as part of Samahang Pilipino, an on-campus organization that focuses on access to higher education and student retention. It was no love at first sight. My carefree, dancing through life attitude didn't mesh with her left brain, analytical thinking approach. However, we rolled in the same social circles and after a summer fling, we grew on each other, eventually becoming an item.

I enrolled as undeclared until I was convinced by everyone else—I was destined to be a doctor. That lasted until my second year, when I tasted Organic Chemistry and pulled all-nighters with lab paperwork. I got out and discovered Biological Anthropology and Asian American studies, not worrying about life after graduation. Maricar started and stuck with Economics because of her parents' insistence–she hated every minute.

We left our university bubble and committed two years to Teach for America (TFA), *dedicating ourselves to high-need schools and becoming lifelong leaders in the effort to end educational inequity*. It guaranteed a paycheck, allowed us to do good and afforded us time to figure out life's purpose.

TFA planted teachers in schools that were typically challenging environments and we got placed in New York City's Bronx. It was trial by fire. For two years, Maricar taught and shined as a math teacher at Knowledge and Power Preparatory Academy III (KAPPA) Middle School, while I tried my best to keep my head above water. It was rough from the beginning. I usually don't cry, but during my first year of teaching, I cried every day. On my morning commute on the 6 train, I thought about quitting constantly, "Is today my last day?" I counted the time down to each weekend and break.

The days off were a necessary outlet and we used them to recharge and explore. On the weekends, we brunched in new neighborhoods, waited in Broadway show lottery lines, or found ourselves in the middle of street festivals.

Being on the East Coast put us within reach of places that were once considered far. Extended weekends were used to take the five-dollar Chinatown bus to visit major cities like Washington DC, Philadelphia, and Boston. For longer breaks, we visited destinations like the Caribbean and hopped across the pond to Europe.

The most uniquely Maricar and James getaway was at the end of May for Memorial Day Weekend. We went to Montauk. Where is, who is and why is Montauk? It's a sleepy beach town, featured in one of our favorite movies, *Eternal Sunshine of a Spotless Mind*–a movie about the inevitability of imperfect relationships and whether memory-erasing is the root of contentment. The most famous line is, "Meet Me in Montauk".

From Penn Station we took the Long Island Rail Road (LIRR) for nearly three hours to see how long the island really was and to find out what was at the end. It was long, and there wasn't much there.

After a day of walking the beaches and a late afternoon cafe lunch, it was time to head back. On a whim, we decided to stay overnight to watch the sunrise. We saw the inflated holiday prices and instead of staying at a hotel like normal adults, we romanticized spending the night on the beach.

The weather took a turn and the temperature dropped, followed by light rain, but we were committed to seeing this through. We bought a large trash bag and a wool blanket from a hardware store and then waited out the rain at a bar, nursing the cheapest drinks possible, water. When we overextended our welcome, we walked to the beach, dug a hole, lined it with the trash bag and then covered ourselves with the blanket. Everything went according to plan except for the most important part–we overslept and missed the sunrise. We caught the next train out and that wrapped up our Montauk experience.

If my students were excited for the end of the year, my enthusiasm was off the charts. I was ready to close this early chapter of my life and start the next. Maricar helped me get through it and I knew she was the one for me. I proposed during our second year of teaching. Obviously, she said "yes."

That summer, at the end of our teaching contract, we drove across the country with two years of our NYC lives packed into a used car. We weaved through cities like Niagara Falls to see the waterfalls (no brainer), Chicago to eat deep dish pizza and *say* hi to MJ, Bloomington to get lost in The Mall of America, and Keystone to behold the most American thing possible, Mount Rushmore. When we finally made it to California, we rekindled friendships before embarking on a five-month trip to explore seven Southeast Asian countries. The timing couldn't have been better. We were young with no responsibilities or expectations, and we used this time of transition to explore beyond our comfort zone. It was liberating.

It was as if this trip was to get *adventure* out of our system since we knew that right around the corner, our priorities would shift to getting real jobs, starting careers and a family, and settling down.

We had a few things planned: our flights to Bali, a return flight to San Francisco via Manila, and a packaged tour from Hanoi to Singapore via STA Travel. We would decide everything else through feel and with the help of our fourth edition of *Lonely Planet Southeast Asia on a Shoestring Budget*. Maricar naturally stepped into the role of trip leader. I followed.

We touched down in Denpasar with our loaded backpacks. A trial run would have been wise because we quickly started to offload a lot of the junk we packed and thought we would need.

Despite traveling in Southeast Asia, where the dollar went much further, we approached this trip with the same frugality we had as teachers. For two years in NYC, we had lived a Spartan lifestyle in a Spanish Harlem apartment, furnished with second hands, and got our daily sustenance from peanut butter and jelly sandwiches. We saved knowing we would need every bit for a house downpayment. We thought:

Why pay $40 for a hotel room when we can get one for $10?

Why eat at a restaurant when we can fill our bellies with street food?

Why pay to enter a UNESCO-recognized temple when plenty of others are free?

Why buy a book when we could exchange our old one? There was always another John Grisham or Stephen King book available that we hadn't yet read.

The adventures we had through our travel-like-a-pauper mentality resulted in the misadventures we replay and laugh about most.

Our first hotel in Denpasar was mosquito-infested and felt like an oven. Everything in the room was worn down because of excessive use and sun exposure. It smelled like incense and mosquito spray, creating a smokey, earthy, and lemony scent. The smells brought me back to the stores I had wandered past along Berkeley's Telegraph Street as a teenager.

We refused to open the screenless windows, fearing an insect attack. To protect ourselves through the night, we layered up and put a blanket over our heads, sealing in the heat as if the humidity weren't enough. It was a miserable first night, and I'm not sure I even slept.

The following day, we assessed the damage. Maricar got the worst of it with a swollen eye and puffed-up lips. Thankfully, we stayed only one night. We were trying to keep costs low, but I made a mental note to raise our housing standards.

The first third of our trip was entirely in Indonesia, and because of our self-imposed budget, we skipped out on hotel food for diner-style, home-cooked meals. I justified this by thinking that we didn't want to fall for the tourist traps and that eating locally would be more authentic.

Adventurous eaters, we were not. We liked Panda Express, stuck to familiar flavors, and preferred Western-style meals.

Indonesian food was a new territory. It had a similar spice profile to Thai and Indian food, but had an added sambal flare. Local restaurants, especially farther away from a town's main strip, become more like open living rooms or *warungs*, a small eatery or cafe. Each warung would prepare several dishes in the morning and put them on display in a glass case. The food did not look familiar and, honestly, not very appetizing. They were mostly stews, and each one was a mystery. These were the days before Google Translate, so we would stand before a display case, eventually rolling the dice on something we hadn't tried before. We'd cross our fingers and point with the other hand. After a few days of this routine, we stuck to the dishes we enjoyed most.

Once we figured out what nasi goreng and mie goreng were, they became daily staples. *Nasi goreng* is Indonesian fried rice, while *mie goreng* is Indonesian fried noodles. They had a spicy kick, and cooks often served them with fresh chili, cucumbers, and a fried egg. There wasn't a day we didn't eat one of these dishes. If Maricar got the noodles, I got the rice, and then we'd switch it up for the next meal. The routine was comforting, knowing what we were getting each time since everything else constantly changed.

After 45 days of trekking from East Java to Jakarta, I was ready to eat anything that wasn't nasi goreng or mie goreng. The capital of Indonesia with millions of people, was the place to break the cycle.

My new favorite became the street food *ayam goreng,* fried chicken. It was a heavenly blend of coriander, turmeric, galangal, and garlic seasonings, served with rice and fresh herbs like what comes on the side of Vietnamese phở. The smell of it would entice me in the same way that an In-and-Out burger would call to me from a mile down the California freeway.

Vendors set up shop on a busy intersection with motorbikes whizzing by, and each created one dish in their makeshift kitchen. Guests would then stand at another station to eat. Whenever we saw a new stand, I made it a point to stop for a bite, thinking I needed to make up for the past month. Maricar, who was overly cautious of street food, refused and stuck to her predictable and safe meals.

We didn't use hand sanitizer then as much as we do now, and there was no running water in these carts. To get around this, customers would use a communal wash bowl where they would dip their hands before eating with those same hands. We were here to blend in, so if it was good enough for everyone else, it was good enough for me. Looking back, that was crazy thinking.

"You know that every time you eat at one of these places, you increase your chance of getting food poisoning?" she said.

"I know. I like to live dangerously," I responded. "And for the record, you're missing out. It tastes so good. How was your mie goreng this morning?"

I needed to reassure myself each time that it was worth the risk.

Maricar gave me a look.

"Just one more time before we fly out. It's a long trip, so you had better eat up."

"I'll pass."

"Your loss."

Right as I took my first bite, I had doubts. I'm unsure if it was the uncooked chicken or a bug I picked up despite using the wash bowl, but I slowly withered away on the flight to Hanoi. If it had been direct, it would have taken six hours, but with our layover, it became a full day of travel.

Maricar looked at me and said, "You don't look so good. This is the first time I've actually seen someone look green."

"Where is the bathroom?"

I feared they wouldn't let me on the plane, and all I wanted to do was hug the toilet. When my stomach wasn't collapsing on itself, I could hear Maricar's voice saying, "I told you so."

I couldn't keep anything in. Things only wanted to come out. I had a narrow escape at the airport and on the plane, hopelessly covering my mouth and barely reaching the toilet. I felt sorry for the people sitting next to me.

After suffering through the plane and taxi rides, I jumped into the hotel bed, closed the door, and didn't come out for days. It was a blur, and all I could remember was a distinct and powerful thirst for lemon-lime Gatorade.

While I suffered, Maricar spent some time contemplating what she would do if my condition worsened. Once she knew I wouldn't die, she spent most of her time enjoying her personal space as she watched entire seasons of *Entourage* and *Sex in the City* on HBO and spent solo walks exploring the culinary scene.

Eventually, I was finally able to sit up without passing out.

"You stink."

I couldn't smell myself, but I'm sure I stank. I was only glad that I could finally get up.

It felt good to shower off the past few days. Getting clean and putting on a new set of clothes helped me take on a positive outlook.

Stepping out of the hotel was a shock as my eyes adjusted to the light. My hearing had decreased from all the scooters, and my breathing labored because of all the smoke.

Recovery went slowly as I had to focus on putting one foot in front of the other. My destination was the health clinic. It wasn't far, but it felt like a journey in my state of atrophied muscles and below-normal calories. The doctor looked at me for five minutes, asked questions, and issued loperamide. I wish I had had this medication earlier rather than suffering and puking everything out over the past few days.

"I thought you were going to die, but now that you are better, let's get something to eat," said Maricar.

"I'd rather not. I would like some lemon-lime Gatorade. I'm craving those electrolytes."

We caught the adventure bug and wouldn't be able to shake it.

Other than my isolating food poisoning experience, Maricar and I were attached to the hip. Some people prefer to travel alone, but I find good company is much better. I always knew that someone had my back, and experiences felt more real, because they were shared.

We made a pretty good team, complementing each other with our contrasting perspectives. While we frequently had different opinions on miscellaneous decisions like whether to eat the chicken or not, our shared life objectives and priorities helped us find common ground when it mattered most.

As we were going from one adventure after the next, I thought to myself that this was a once-in-a-lifetime experience, and I'm glad that we were able to create them. I was sharing each of them with someone I knew I would be with for the rest of my life, and I would have them forever.

When it was time to return to America, it felt like we had been gone for years. The dream holiday was ending, and I was excited to get started with life.

"Maricar, promise me we'll do something like this again when we grow up."

"You're being so cheesy!"

"I'm serious! After we have kids and retire, let's travel the world."

"Alright, I promise... but it's a long way off. Just make sure you don't get tired on me or forget."

"Ditto."

We were able to have this early life adventure because we had the freedom, the means and the drive.

What happens when life gets in the way?

What type of responsibilities will be on our plate? Will we be too busy?

What will life be like after kids? Will we have different priorities?

Where will we be financially and how much is enough to go on an adventure?

These are questions we would soon answer.

PART ONE
REDEFINING OUR PATH

Challenging the conventional route and embracing an alternative path that enables us to be fully engaged, crafting unforgettable moments together.

1

IS THIS SOMETHING YOU WILL REGRET?

November 2013

When Maricar and I first discussed kids, we wanted a big family and thought five was perfect. Of course, this was before we had even just one.

Jero came along in 2009, and we stopped sleeping. Co-sleeping, sandwiching him between us every night, might work for other families, but not for us. At first, it was nice, but then he became dependent and couldn't sleep unless someone was with him. Having an extra body in the bed compromised our sleep quality.

How can you pick out a new parent from a lineup? They all have that distinctive "I-haven't-slept-in-months" look. It wears down the body, and new parents become zombies for at least a year. Our dream of a basketball team of kids quickly changed and we would be happy with just a mixed doubles tennis pair.

Two years later, in 2011, Lea arrived. We had one of each, and now, a complete set.

We went from one parenting extreme to another, refusing to operate in the gray. As soon as Lea hit four months, we taught her to sleep independently using the "cry-it-out" method. For those uninitiated, you leave your four-month-old in her crib, checking in after progressively longer periods but never rushing to pick her up. It teaches independence. If you give in—all it takes is one weak parent—it teaches her that if she can cry long enough, someone will come to the rescue.

Because of the cry-it-out method, we were all soon sleeping through the night. Of course, we didn't get off easy since Lea was a handful in many other ways. She had been exclusively breastfed while Maricar was on maternity leave. When it was time for Maricar to return to teaching, Lea needed to learn how to bottle-feed, but she had absolutely no interest in acquiring that skill. Just like with sleeping, we had to draw the line for everyone's long-term well-being. Recommended by her pediatrician, the plan was to starve her until she came around. You can't beat the instinct to eat, right?

She was so stubborn that she held off for a whole day and refused to stop crying. She won. Her grandparents brought her to KIPP Summit Academy, a 45-minute drive from our house, for an emergency feeding during Maricar's lunch break.

Our family got into a nice rhythm as Lea approached her second birthday. Jero was becoming more independent with the biggest win of his life up to this point: potty training. We bribed him. For every successful potty, he got rewarded with a train. It didn't take him long to collect Thomas and all his friends.

The rough parts were over. It was a blur, but we got through it. Did I want to do it again? No. I was ready to move on and enjoy life with our little humans.

And then, we had *the talk*.

We were both in Lea's room putting away toys and items she'd already outgrown into the donation box. I popped the question.

"Lea's almost two. Think it's time to donate the crib and get her a real bed?"

I tried to ask the question as casually as possible and held my breath, knowing my seemingly innocent question was loaded. We had been putting off this conversation for at least a year.

"Are you implying that we are done?"

"Well, yeah. That's what I thought." We had already donated most of the baby clothes and countless newborn items. And now, it was time for the crib.

I felt like we were done having kids. After getting through the most challenging years, I looked forward to raising the kids we have and having more personal time.

I should have expected this. There were signs that Maricar wanted another. Every time we donated an item, she would get sentimental and replay memories. I was the opposite, constantly looking forward and thinking about what was next.

Maricar shared, "I've been thinking about it, and I want a third. I know it's silly since Jero and Lea are still babies, but I feel like it happened so quickly. Almost like I missed it."

I thought, *she's not making sense*. It's like the illogical choices after running a marathon. One quickly forgets about the suffering they just went through, the countless times they said, "I'll never do this again," only to sign up for another one mere moments after they finish while high on endorphins. The next week, when training starts, reality sets in.

Why did I sign up for this thing again?

By pushing back, I thought I was doing us a favor.

Anticipating that this conversation would come up, I brought out my best rhetorical questions and comments from my back pocket.

"Do you want to go backwards and change diapers?"

"We would have to rebuy all the stuff we just got rid of."

"I like my sleep."

"If we have another, we aren't going to be able to travel."

"Why screw up a good thing?"

She didn't give me any response.

It was an ordinary wooden crib, but we both knew what was at stake. It was a defining moment, forcing us to decide the type of family we wanted and the lifestyle that followed.

I'm practical.

America is designed for families of four. Hotels have two queen beds. Cars are made for two people in the back—that middle seat doesn't count—and it was easier to schedule play dates because there were only two kids to match. And when it came to supervision, we played zone defense with one and then switched to a doable man-to-man with two. Three kids would outnumber us, and we would have to switch back to the zone, constantly feeling like we were missing something.

Having a third would also mean more sleepless nights, additional years of changing diapers, and figuring out how to make life work. I didn't want that.

We had a set, and we were complete.

She said, "I want a third. I want Lea to have a younger sibling. I want to have a few extra years to hold them. I miss that baby smell. I want to know what their personality will be like."

Maricar finished her closing statement.

"In 20 years, what would you regret more: having another or not?"

She had a point and got her way.

In making the decision, I thought about the past four years. Was it the lack of sleep? Was I overly focused on getting to the end of the tunnel? Did I believe the grass was greener on the other side a year from now?

The crib was a wake-up call that I needed to be present and savor these moments as a parent. They were flying by, and although I couldn't return in time, I could get a do-over with a third and be a more present father moving forward.

We got to work, and in September 2014, we had Feris.

Having a third kid brought us closer together out of necessity. We were happy to host and invite others, but we would rarely be invited because the sheer number of a party of five becomes overwhelming.

Jero and Lea enjoyed having a younger sister that they could care for. Jero continued to get an unfair amount of attention because he was the eldest and only boy. And Lea liked a younger sibling who would follow her around and obey her. She now had a sidekick and enjoyed being the boss.

"I am the queen. Get me my drink!" Lea would say. "I am the queen. Get me my drink!" Feris would repeat.

With Feris in the house, silence was a thing of the past, and I couldn't envision a life without her. This also marked the end of our travel days and it seemed unlikely that we would embark on new adventures anytime soon.

2
LIFE ON TRACK

May 2014

Life is busy, but the hustle is all worth it in the end.

Work took most of the day, and even when it was done, it was still top of mind.

I had a morning commute that would start with a 20-minute bike ride to BART, the San Francisco Bay Area Rapid Transit system. I would wait 5-10 minutes on the platform before hopping on a 50-minute train ride from Dublin/Pleasanton, the end of the line, to New Montgomery station in San Francisco. At least ten minutes of guaranteed delays were expected from a medical emergency, police activity at Fruitvale station, or a mechanical issue. The final stretch was a five-minute walk to my office. That was one way. Round trip, this commute took up three hours every weekday.

At first, I would complain about the commute and the smells of the city and become irritated every time there was a delay. That didn't help because there was a delay every day. Then, I accepted it all and recognized it as a suburb tax that people paid for more space, safety, and better schools. We lived in San Ramon, on the edge of the Bay Area, and the toll was high.

I had roughly 12 hours at home, which was eaten up by sleep, ferrying kids to after school commitments, errands, and chores.

With Feris arriving in a few months, I carried these numbers and fatigue into my annual self-reflection session. It is the time of the year when I ask myself, *is this the life I want?*

In my late 20s, a manager introduced me to a life-visualization exercise that took me beyond the day-to-day responsibilities, helped me focus on the things that mattered, and encouraged free-flow storytelling.

Here was the prompt:

Imagine you bump into a close friend you haven't seen in ten years. She asks, "What have you been up to?" You have 20 minutes to answer her question. Record yourself.

When I ask this question in the present tense, it helps me clarify my life. It distracts me from the daily, weekly, and monthly to-do checklists and helps me visualize the big picture: the goals I'm working towards, the milestones I want to reach, and the passions that bring me joy.

Afterward, I would listen to the tape and ask myself:

"Is this the life I'm proud to live? Is this what I envisioned for myself? What would I change? Where did I stretch the truth or straight out lie?"

An equally powerful alternative to this exercise is to imagine the same scenario, except you bump into that same friend ten or twenty years into the future.

What makes this different is that your future still needs to be written, and your actions today will determine if this imagined future state comes true.

It was 2014. Each year I've had this conversation with myself, it has been more or less the same, and I saw that as a good thing. I had created a plan that was playing out as I wanted. All I had to do was stay on the path, and everything would work out.

Here was a sampling of life thoughts and highlights:

I am in my prime, working for a fun, relevant company and our projects are impactful. I get paid well and build out cool development programs for managers and leaders. We've scaled quickly, survived the financial crisis, and are no longer a startup. Maricar is thriving as a middle school teacher, loving what she does, and getting praised constantly by admin, her peers, students and even parents. She's a celebrity in the San Ramon Windemere community.

Maricar and I celebrated our fifth wedding anniversary with a family trip to Hawaii this past summer. We moved into our forever home in a great neighborhood close to friends and family. For a while, I had been competing in triathlons, but I switched exclusively to running because of time. Now that the kids sleep through the night, I feel better. Our third is on the way, and I'm certain this will be our last one.

Jero, our eldest, is in kindergarten, and Lea, our daughter, is in preschool full-time. We pile more activities to their plate to build up their resume. To give the kids a head start, financial costs have added up. We should be doing a better job staying connected with friends from high school and college. Family parties and gatherings feel like a revolving door, and we rush to get from one place to another.

Overall, everything is on track as we imagined it would be. If we keep doing what we are doing, we will retire well and set the kids up for a future to do whatever they want.

This is how I answered the question about what I thought my life would look like 20 years into the future. For context, I would be about 50, and the kids would be 24, 22, and 19.

Our twenty-fifth wedding anniversary is coming up and we will celebrate in Italy. It has been on our bucket list and the whole trip will revolve around food. We've been living in the same house, planting strong roots, and building relationships. Through our discipline, the mortgage is paid off and we've had extra money to remodel the bathrooms and kitchen. Our fruit trees are fully mature and thriving.

We are now empty nesters, but our kids visit monthly for dinner and special occasions. It doesn't happen as often as we would like, but we're thankful when we are all together. We go on an annual family trip. And because we foot the bill, the kids are happy to come. I hope this isn't the only reason.

We are still maxing out our 401(k), retirement account, and don't consider ourselves rich but we are comfortable and don't worry about money. The peace of mind is wonderful.

With our extra time, we volunteer at our local animal shelter. We replaced the kids with a chocolate labrador.

I've switched back to triathlons and finished my first Ironman a few years ago. I do one a year with a few shorter distances sprinkled in. I'm looking to get into destination events.

Retirement is only 15 years away.

Listening to the recording, I thought this was all shaping up to be a good life. I needed no major moves or Herculean efforts to make the plan come to fruition.

All we had to do was stick to the plan, not do anything stupid, and everything would play out as scripted. Life was good.

I noticed myself saying "on track" repeatedly.

What did it mean to be "on track?" When did I decide this was the path I would follow?

My parents immigrated from the Philippines to California in the early 70s for better opportunities and to achieve the American Dream. A belief that if you paid your dues, you were guaranteed financial security, success, and happiness. They were the typical Pilipino stereotype, securing stable, recession proof jobs. My dad, Joseph, worked for the US Post Office and my mom, Rebecca, was a nurse.

They came from humble beginnings and worked hard. I don't remember them ever taking a sick day, sitting down to relax, or taking time for themselves. If they weren't at work pulling a double, they were fixing, repairing, or preparing something for our benefit.

I was born and raised in East Oakland's Jefferson neighborhood with my two brothers, Jenner and Jeff. In the early 80s, this was not the place you wanted to raise a family. The local elementary, middle and high school have a GreatSchools rating of 3, 2, and 2 respectively and someone would break into our house every few months.

I never thought we were poor, although, I knew not to ask for stuff. My mom would share heartbreaking stories of taking us to Kmart, a retail chain, to browse the toy aisles, knowing that she couldn't afford to buy us anything. Fishing and crabbing at the Berkeley pier were regular pastimes and our default holiday was going to a nearby campground in our iconic white top, red bottom Volkswagen van.

I remember these fondly as good times.

When my mom passed her nursing exam that allowed her to go from a Licensed Vocational Nurse (LVN) to a Registered Nurse (RN) with twice the pay, our lives got upgraded. We moved to El Sobrante, a huge step up in safety, and money suddenly wasn't so tight.

As a kid, I knew we had enough and it couldn't have been that bad since my parents managed to send us to the local Catholic schools, we always had food on the table, and we had everything we needed. They provided all this to put my brothers and me in a better position to achieve the dream. It was working. I bought into their vision and inherited their path, building on their sacrifices through hard work and getting closer to the promised land.

This annual reflection exercise reassured me that I was on a proven trajectory. By discipline, like my parents, I could hold off on eating the marshmallow now and then get rewarded with two or maybe three down the line. I was always good at this.

At the same time, I felt doubt. It might result from watching *The Matrix* one too many times, believing that we are just a cog serving someone else's agenda, and relying too much on society to tell me what I should do and value.

From my responses, I prioritized two things:

First, I prioritized security and making decisions that avoided missteps and surprises.

Second, I prioritized significance and finding ways to be relevant and an important member of society.

Because of these values and my commitment to carrying on my parents' plan, there were compromises and sacrifices I had made that didn't get reported on the balance sheet or the annual life update:

How much time did I spend away from my family? What was I giving up?

Where was my energy spent? Who did I give the best version of myself to?

How will my kids remember me and what example do I want to set?

It got me thinking.

What if instead of following a path that was focused on moving on up, I focused on the now, being present and connecting with my family?

What if I already had enough and was financially content, how would I structure my life differently?

I didn't know what this alternative would look like, how I would get it, or if I even had it in me to make the shift. At this point in my life, I was heads down with blinders, pushing forward to get through it because I thought that was what I was supposed to do.

Knowing that I got this far, it was easier to stay on the path. I might as well keep going. There's a phrase for this exact thinking: a sunk-cost fallacy. It occurs when a person sticks with a decision primarily because they have invested so much time and resources into it. But it wasn't just me. It was my parents, and their parents that believed in this dream and worked so hard to achieve it.

I wasn't having a midlife crisis, but I was asking the questions that planted the seeds of doubt. It encouraged me to think outside the box. I didn't have the answers or the guts to pull it off yet, but the wheels were in motion.

3
WHAT IS YOUR DREAM VACATION?

August 2017

"It's official. We've entered the golden age of parenting," I said.

"Huh? What are you talking about?" asked Maricar.

"The golden age of parenting. It's when your kid, or in our case, kids, are old enough to be out of diapers but young enough that they still want to hang out with their parents. With Feris successfully using the toilet three times in a row, we made it!"

"I don't believe you. Did you make this up?"

Maricar knows she should take everything I say with a grain of salt. Sometimes, I draw from a recent conversation, pull something from the internet, or make it up. In this case, I picked up this idea from a friend, a decade older than us. His kids are in their late teens, and he couldn't wait to get them out of the house.

"Who cares if I made it up or not? It makes sense, right? It only lasts a few years, so we've got to make the most of it."

"What did you have in mind?"

Whenever we had information to bring to the table, we thought about how to use it, and this was no exception. We used this as an opportunity to take a holiday we've been putting off.

"What about Antarctica?"

I'm already doing the back of the napkin math, and my napkin tells me Antarctica will cost a fortune. And for what? To see some penguins and get bragging rights for Instagram? Opening up the conversation, we explore other options.

"We could do that. Anything else?"

"An African safari? Palawan? The Great Barrier Reef? Fiji? Iceland?"

"These all sound great, but remember, Feris is still a toddler. I don't want to have to carry her up a mountain or save her from a shark. Maybe these are trips we could take when the kids get older or at the very least, things we could do on our own when we retire."

"How about the Alaskan Disney Cruise? We bring it up at least once a year, and depending on when we go, Feris should remember it. If we are going all out, we can even invite both grandparents since eating, cruising, and sleeping seem to be their favorite pastimes these days."

I'm a huge fan of Disney because of their attention to detail, and I knew if we could figure out the logistics to make it happen, it would be the best vacation ever. Having both sets of healthy grandparents in an environment that worked for everyone would be a dream come true.

"I'm on board. Let's make it happen. What's next?"

We looked at the sailing schedule and picked a date during the summer break that worked for everyone. To bookend the trip, we added a road trip to and from the Vancouver port, a total of 2,000 miles of driving from San Francisco. My mom even got everyone matching T-shirts, so it was clear to everyone else we were on holiday.

We learned a few important lessons.

Lesson one: Timing matters.

Why can the same experience fall flat for one person but be life-changing for another? It's all in the timing.

With three kids and aging grandparents, there is a finite window of time for these experiences. If we had gone a year earlier, not only would we have needed a bag dedicated to diapers, but Feris might not even have remembered going on this trip. If we went a year later, I know Jero wouldn't have had the same enthusiasm, potentially aging out of many activities.

Lesson two: There must be something for everyone.

A cruise catered to our diverse preferences ranging from a three-year-old to a recent retiree. If one wants to eat and sleep all day, that option is available. Fortunately, the grandparents still had that go-go mentality. They were excited to be active and take advantage of everything the cruise offered, even going on the occasional off-ship excursion.

Even if this concept of the perfect parenting window was make-believe, it got us thinking:

What activities and experiences can we and should we take advantage of right now?

For any experience, is there a perfect window for it?

Lesson three: It all starts with a decision.

Ever since hearing about the Alaskan Disney Cruise and the five-star experiences of families, we knew we wanted to do it. We believed there would always be a reason to do it later or an excuse to never do it, so we fully committed, and everything fell into place. If there were an obstacle, such as getting the days off or figuring out how to get from one place to the next, we'd take care of it. Going from talking about doing something to doing it was a massive shift in mindset, and it was empowering to know what we could accomplish.

By nature, we would have worked out the details and laid out all options, considering outcomes before making a well-informed and concrete decision. It was the right way. What we were beginning to understand, which they don't teach you in school, is that in life, the *how* often starts falling into place after you decide. Sometimes you must make that decision *before* you have all the information.

In a previous life, I would have considered this approach irresponsible or rash, but from where I was at that time, the mistake was in taking too long or never deciding. I didn't want to miss an opportunity where we could all be together.

What do you want?

It's an open-ended question that invites bold thinking. We started asking it more after this trip. What if we never posed the question? Can you imagine if we missed out because we didn't think bigger?

Just like in the movie *Tangled*, when Rapunzel makes her dream come true by seeing the floating lanterns, she sets her sights on a new goal. That's what we were doing. We asked, *What else?*

But the difference this time is that it wasn't just an exercise. Because we manufactured our own urgency and we knew that we had the skills to execute, we thought of this as an action list rather than a wish list.

In Their Words:
The Disney Alaskan Cruise

Dr. Seuss once said, "Sometimes you will never know the value of a **moment**, until it becomes a memory."

"In Their Words" is a section added to select chapters where Jero, Lea, and Feris share their unfiltered opinions about what they remember about a given time or place. See the Author's Note for more details.

Jero (8):

- *I was especially excited because we could hang out with both grandparents. I got to ride in Papa Joker's van and I was so excited it was hard for me to fall asleep. I kept getting confused between Canada and Russia. I thought we were going to see an igloo.*
- *Up to this point, we had been gluten-free. However, Mommy said that we could take a break from the diet for two weeks while we were on vacation. It was our first time having muffins, breads, and croissants in a long time.*
- *This was 2018, and* The Avengers: Infinity War *had just come out. They had a fancy movie theater on the boat, and we got to watch it again and again.*
- *To get on the boat, you have to have an ID card. I remember I was excited because it had all my information. When we were*

walking back to the boat, I remember taking it out and playing with it. I dropped my card, and it slipped between the cracks and fell into the water. I started crying because my parents convinced me that I wouldn't be able to get back on the boat. I still have the replacement card.

Lea (6):

- *As a souvenir, I got an Arctic wolf animal stuffed animal with beads.*
- *There was a kids' club area where we would get dropped off. They had games, but I thought it was boring because they let kids do whatever they wanted.*
- *There was a lot of chocolate syrup in all the breakfast items. I liked the Disney waffles with Mickey's face the best. And because it was a buffet, I could get as much as I wanted.*
- *There was a* Frozen *show with Anna and Elsa. At the end of the show, they had a fake snow machine that blew all over the place. I thought it was cool.*
- *We all wore the same red shirts as souvenirs.*
- *Every day, they would fix our room and fold the towels into origami creatures. They also included a yummy chocolate.*

Feris (3):

- *I cried in the kids' club. I don't know why.*
- *There were a lot of fun things to do, like the water slide.*

4
OUR TIPPING POINT

November 2018

Back in July, we got a save-the-date for a destination wedding in Rome. It was from Maricar's best friend from college.

"Should we go?" she asked.

For every reason to go, there was an equally good reason to say no. It all depended on what we wanted to do.

"What about the kids?"

"They can stay with your parents."

"What about work?"

"I'll request those days off."

"What about Thanksgiving?"

"Who cares?"

"And what about _____?"

"We'll figure that out, too."

"Let's do it!"

Entrepreneur Jim Rohn once said, "If you really want to do something, you'll find a way. If you don't, you'll find an excuse." True.

Riding our seize-the-day attitude, we decided to find a way to make it happen. We were saying yes to choices we wanted to make in the past but would fall to the wayside over endless conversations.

Once we decided to go, everything else was easy. Our kids were a bit older now, and we didn't feel guilty leaving them behind. They were easy, and we had family who we could trust.

It really was everything else, including the social norms of what you should do over the holidays. Those expectations took more work to navigate.

Holidays, regardless of the celebration, are a big deal in my extended family. You are expected to show up.

I grew up with nearly two dozen first cousins who celebrated everything together since we were born, from birthdays and piano recitals to all the holidays. Not showing up was not an option.

You didn't want to be that guy.

"Where is ___? What does he have going on? Too good for us this year?"

We always showed up and often hosted bigger events like Christmas. Why? As soon as Jero was born, we wanted to build traditions they could lock into their memories and look forward to. We wanted simple traditions like picking out a tree and decorating it the day after Thanksgiving or going for a family bike ride around the neighborhood on Christmas Eve.

We would break tradition this one time.

Talking with my parents and family helped get the load off my chest. I felt guilty at first but then switched my focus to why we were doing this and the unique opportunity ahead of us.

It was our Roman holiday, sans kids.

At 35, we felt like we had secured our place in the world and weren't afraid of a little adventure. Okay, we weren't in our 20s, and anything past 9 p.m. was late, but we still had many good years in us until we got to the point of exploring through a bus window or a cruise ship.

I'd be lying if I said we went just for the wedding. It gave us a chance to do something different, something off-script. We appreciated this opportunity and knew we had to make the most of these ten days.

The flight from San Francisco to Rome was over 12 hours long. We landed in the late afternoon, and once in Rome, we hit the ground running, literally. Maricar and I went for a run to fight off jet lag before we met up with our friends. With no cell service, we played it safe and ran an out-and-back 5k, using the river as a compass. If we were along the river, I thought, we couldn't get lost.

"How about we go a little further?"

"It looks like there is a soccer game going on. Let's check it out."

"What's over that hill?"

"Let's see."

On my home turf, I run the same loop every day. I know exactly how many steps I need to make before the next turn and the pace I need to run to hit my splits, so I finish within seconds of my predicted time. With new surroundings, I get curious. It's probably why Maricar gets frustrated and hesitates on a James run in new territory. She likes to know where we are running, how far, and how fast. That mixed with my casual and adventurous vacation attitude is like water and oil.

It started to get dark quickly, and we found ourselves lost, without money, a phone, or the ability to speak Italian. Maricar is naturally more responsible and has a great sense of direction. Getting lost never happens when I'm with her because she either talks me out of doing something impulsive or saves the day and leads us home. This was not one of those times. We were lost.

"We'll just ask for help."

This didn't work. The farther we got from tourist central, the fewer people understood English. And based on the looks we were getting when asking for help, we were far from home.

We popped into a small cafe and tried our best to get directions. Not helpful. And because we were staying at an Airbnb, we couldn't name-drop a hotel. With famous landmarks everywhere, you would think we would have memorized at least one near our place.

The frustration set in, and I was getting worried. Maricar was already giving me that look I'm all too familiar with.

What now?

We backtracked and found a bus stop with a map.

"Oh, that's where we are?"

I hadn't realized we had come that far, but it was clear what happened. It looked like the river snakes around, and with all our crisscrossing, I lost which direction was north.

Eventually, we made it back. Our short 5k welcome to Rome turned into a 20k-*Amazing Race* challenge. We slept like babies that night and had no problems with jetlag. Like I always say, it all works out in the end.

We spent, at most, half a day with friends. It wasn't for the lack of trying. It's just that everyone seemed to have their agenda of what they wanted to see and do. We were all close friends at one point but had drifted apart since university. When we first touched down in Rome, I thought the point was to be together, away from the distractions that created distance between us back home.

The bride and groom were focused on the wedding. Then, after tying the knot, they were off on their honeymoon.

Another couple brought their toddler, and you know how that is.

One was a world traveler and had gone to Rome before, so she was off to Paris after the festivities.

And so, it goes.

Maybe it was my fault. I was trying to relive the university days when time wasn't a problem. The boredom from all the downtime created spontaneity and resulted in some of the most unique and memorable experiences. The days of carefree attitudes, going with the flow, and seeing where each experience leads were behind us. We were all now grown up, and God forbid we would be caught without a plan. Everyone had their own lives now.

Unless there was a point person to bring everyone together and lay out an agenda, people would splinter off. I would see instances of this splintering applying equally to friends and family, to the point that what was once a close relationship fizzles into just another acquaintance you send a holiday card to once a year.

We were not the exception. Maricar and I had each other and were driven to see and do as much as we could, not knowing if we'd ever be back.

Our few days here felt like a month. From Rome, we went to Florence, Venice, and then Cinque Terre before returning back.

Note that just because other people like it doesn't mean you will. In Venice, it's supposedly all about seafood. Maricar looks up the most popular place to get seafood pasta and orders it. I took one whiff.

"It's all yours. Enjoy."

When Maricar and I were in college, we spent a summer studying at the University of Hawai'i–West O'ahu. One day, we rented scooters with our friends and toured Honolulu. It was so much fun, and we wanted to relive it in Florence.

I thought, *it's just like riding a bike. You never forget, right?*

It had been at least ten years since I've driven one of these things. *Was I going to be alright?*

The owner of the shop was convincing in his Italian accent.

"If you know how to ride a bike, you'll be fine. Why don't you take the scooter out on a short ride? Get a feel for how it handles before your wife hops on the back?"

"Good idea."

"I got this."

Within two minutes of pulling out of the driveway, I panicked because I was on a main road, traveling farther from the familiar part of town and into more congestion. I was trying to keep the bike upright and not get in an accident, so figuring out how to turn was out of the question. Flashbacks of our recent run came back. Now, the situation was worse because I was operating a traffic accident waiting to happen.

Fearing I would get lost weaving through streets, I found an opening and pulled an illegal U-turn. In the process, I dropped the scooter in the middle of a busy road with oncoming traffic coming from both directions. I thought, *well, that's the end of this ride.* At least I tried. As cars passed and honked, I could feel the sweat start to trickle down my back and the shame from embarrassment.

I muscled the scooter upright, hopped on, and returned to the rental place. It was only a ten-minute ride, but I felt a huge relief when I returned.

Do we call off the ride? How much should I tell Maricar? Will it do any good?

I decided to be honest and use my nonchalant, confident voice.

"What took you so long?"

"I got lost, and I couldn't figure out when I could turn around, so I just kept going."

I then whispered, "I also dropped the bike."

"Is it okay to ride?"

"I think so. We just need to get out of this congested area. Once we are on the open road, I'll be fine."

The shop recommended a route that would take us through Florence's downtown and then across the Arno River to take in the views from Piazzale Michelangelo and see the Tuscany countryside.

It sounded fantastic, and it would have been if the weather had been nice.

At this point in the year, the Italian countryside had gone dormant, and we had to imagine what this place would look and feel like in all its summer glory.

Scootering around in unfamiliar territory at 40 miles per hour and traveling in the cold with the chance of heavy rain showers made a huge difference. That combination turned the weather from chilly to teeth-chattering ice cold. Even though we layered up with everything we brought, it still wasn't enough.

We looked out of place because of our attire as the only tourists on a scooter. Imagine Harry and Lloyd making the trip to Aspen on a 50cc. We were shivering messes.

There wasn't anything extraordinary we saw or that happened on the ride, however, it was an experience that exceeded our usual boundaries and ventured beyond what we would typically consider doing. This made it unforgettable.

Italy is a common destination on many people's bucket lists. Some individuals take it a step further by including famous cities like Venice, Milan, or Florence, which are often part of a ten-day European tour. As someone who had always dreamed of visiting Italy (but hadn't taken the next step), Cinque Terre, our final Italian city, was a wonderful surprise.

To get there, we made a lot of train transfers. And, because we were traveling in the off-season, most stores and hiking trails were closed due to unpredictable weather. We used this to our advantage and slowed down. Rather than an itinerary filled with checkboxes, our open schedule allowed us to soak in the surrounding beautiful cliffs and calming sea.

There were no dinner reservations, shows we needed to catch, or standing in line. We spent an afternoon taking our time to walk down to the promenade and sat on a bench longer than usual. We appreciated the weather when it would clear up for an hour and were grateful when a small market was open, so we didn't starve. It was a nice pace change from the rest of our trip and even our lives.

With our recent experience on the Alaskan Disney Cruise and already questioning our life path for a while, we were primed and looking for adventure. This Italian experience was significant and life changing because of its timing, giving us a taste of life beyond the American Dream and what it had to offer. It tipped the scales, shifting our mentality of "what if" to "how can we". There were several key insights that brought about that change.

Once in Italy, everything that was once impossible suddenly became accessible. The challenge was clearing the hurdle of getting there. Then, we had experiences available for us to enjoy now, not 20 years from now. By drastically changing our surroundings, a whole new world of possibilities opened up.

Everything that tourists say about Italy is true. It is truly wonderful. The prices for accommodation, food, and getting around were shockingly affordable. Our dollars went so much further abroad. For so long, I thought it wasn't in our budget.

What if we had decided not to take the trip? Would we know what we were missing? How many more experiences would we get like this?

We welcomed the change of pace without the kids, but we missed them. We wished they could see and experience everything we went through. Telling them the stories and showing countless pictures wasn't enough. I wanted to share these experiences with them. I wanted to see how they would react and what they would remember. I wanted to be able to relive the moments and have them contribute to the story.

Do you remember the movie *Contact*? In the end, when Ellie, played by Jodie Foster, jumped through the portal, she was away for a split second but got an experience that was 18 hours.

Did we find the secret to a long life? By getting out of the routine and creating distinct memories, our concept of time expanded. Rather than time being one big lump, parts of the day became distinct stand-alone events.

We saw a glimpse of a different life and couldn't stop thinking about it—a life where we redefined our understanding of what was normal, changed the setting, and made each day an adventure.

Knowing that we'd get overwhelmed with our everyday life checklists when we got home, we said no to movies and no to sleep on the plane. Instead, we enthusiastically used the long-haul flight to discuss what this alternative reality would look like and, more importantly, how we could make it happen.

Somewhere inside, we had already made the decision we were doing this.

5
WE JUST NEED ONE YES

January 2019

All we needed was one opportunity to put this idea of a life abroad into motion.

Maricar and I used the plane ride from Rome to start the discussion and used the week to play them out.

"If we were to move abroad, what would it look like?"

"Was now the time?"

"Do we have enough money?"

"When would we go? For how long?"

"What about work? Could we just leave?"

"What about our kids' education?"

"What about everything we've built? If we leave, are we giving up on that dream?"

If we weren't serious, we would table the conversation and revisit it in six months. That's the practical option. Instead, we blocked out the time now.

Like many of life's forks in the road, we had questions and few answers. We fell back on recent lessons that timing mattered a lot.

First, our plans had to align with the school academic calendar to minimize the impact on the kids' education and Maricar's work.

Second, we wanted to make this happen within the next two years before the kids were in middle school. If we waited too long, we'd get pushback from the kids, and the impact on their education and social well-being could be disastrous.

Our self-imposed perfect window to make this happen was open now. Why?

Jero, the eldest, was nine and still a few years from middle school. Lea, seven, was right in the middle. Feris was four, potty trained, and trying to keep up with her older siblings.

If we had gone when they were babies, they would have been too fragile, and we would have had to lug around all the accessories that come with them. They also probably wouldn't have remembered anything. If we waited too long, we would all have been constantly at each other's throats. Traveling provides enough stress. We didn't need to add teenage hormones to the mix.

During the most recent summer, we saw ideal timing come together with the Disney Alaskan Cruise, and we wanted to continue to take advantage. We created urgency and wanted to go all in on fostering more shared memorable experiences to help us come closer as a family.

Having a purpose and a call to immediate action was the perfect fuel combination as we continued our mission. We researched and had conversations to better understand what this adventure would be like. Our options were the following:

Option One: Take a one-year work sabbatical. We would rent out our house, homeschool the kids, and travel worldwide.

- Action Items: Map out the one-year travel destinations and logistics. Create a budget and school curriculum.
- Pros: This would be the dream.
- Cons: The cost of traveling nonstop for a year; planning logistics for a yearlong trip.

Option Two: Maricar gets a placement through the Department of Defense Schools (DODS).

- Action Items: Complete application requirements.
- Pros: Education and housing are free. Transitioning to an American school abroad and a base is easy.
- Cons: Reservations working for the military because of ideological beliefs and concerns regarding the use of force and violence. The application process takes years.

Option Three: Maricar gets a job at an international school.

- Action Items: Sign up for a recruiting agency and apply for jobs.
- Pros: Kids get a first-class education. Exposure to a diverse community.
- Cons: A teacher with four dependents (i.e., a spouse and three kids) would not be an ideal hire. In most cases, an international school would only partially cover tuition, meaning we'd have to cover the rest.

Option Four: We don't take the adventure of a lifetime.

- Action Items: None.
- Pros: Nothing changes.
- Cons: Nothing changes.

We weighed the options. *If we wanted to do this, we had to cast a wide net.*

I looked into finances and logistics while Maricar started the application process.

To increase our chances, we considered my options for also working abroad. The goal was to be free of commitments, not live our current life abroad. An international work assignment was a slippery slope, imposing many of the same demands that kept me busy, limiting our travel opportunities and overall quality of life. The other alternative was for me to teach. Although I had my degree, two traumatic years of teaching middle school were enough to scar me for life. I swore never to go back to the classroom unless absolutely necessary.

We decided that I would take care of our household and well-being. I would also fill in financially if we were in the red with our spending. It required me to wear a full-time domestic hat and focus on our greater vision.

Maricar was the talent and gem of our household. She had a heavier load. I wondered if she knew the role she was stepping into, of leader and breadwinner. Regardless, she moved forward, determined to make this work.

Financially, we weren't in a position to responsibly take a year off. It was possible, but it would put us in a tight position, and I feared it would haunt us the whole time. If the other opportunities didn't pan out, we decided to take this as a last resort.

"To qualify as a Department of Defense middle school math teacher, I need to take additional higher-level math. I haven't done calculus since my first year of college. Should I sign up?"

"Yes."

"Should I join Search Associates? There's a fee but they help me with my application and help me get a placement."

"Yes."

"There's an upcoming job fair. Is it worth it to go?"

"Yes."

My job was to support Maricar and reassure her that everything she did increased our chances. In my mind, it was all worth it. At this time, I also carried a heavier load of family responsibilities, protecting her from distractions. I was happy to play the role because I knew I couldn't do what she was doing.

Things were moving quickly, and we kept an open mind. We came into the process late in the cycle and set high expectations as motivators but were kind to ourselves if things didn't work out. After all, it was more than likely that nothing would change, but we could at least dream. It happened a lot over the next few weeks. For every school Maricar applied to, we'd read about their academics and drool over the facilities and the opportunities it would provide us.

"Check out this school in Taiwan."

"Where is Taiwan? Is that next to Japan?"

"Sure."

We were naive and didn't know what to look for. We could convince ourselves that anything was a good destination if it fit our minimum criteria. As a partner giving my two cents, I felt like I was trying to fill out a college basketball March Madness tournament bracket and choosing teams to win based on mascots and team colors.

The following list gives you a sample of the schools around the world Maricar applied to:

DOD Schools (all over Germany, Japan)
Stamford American (Hong Kong)
Dulwich College (Seoul)
American School in Japan
American School of the Hague (Netherlands)
Cheonga Dalton (South Korea)
International School of Brussels
John F. Kennedy School (Berlin)
International Bilingual School at Hsinchu Park (Taiwan)
Korea International (Jeju)
International School Mainfranken (Schweinfurt Germany)
International School of Aruba
International School of Amsterdam
Cayman International School
Uruguayan American School
Shattuck St. Mary's (Malaysia)

Suito Kokusi High school (Osaka)

After Maricar applied to a school, she would most often receive only an automated "Thank you for your application." However, there were a few opportunities where we got our hopes up, only for them to be crushed days later. An international school in Taiwan gave a verbal offer and rescinded it a day later when the departing teacher decided to return. Another school in Japan, which Maricar had high hopes for and even created a custom video for, bluntly advised us we wouldn't be able to afford Tokyo with three kids. That rejection hurt because it was a reminder of our reality.

After each no, Maricar would take a day to process the news before bouncing right back.

We kept the whole process quiet from family and friends, and shared only some information with the kids. The kids saw things as black and white. When we showed them a school, they couldn't help but conclude it would be their new school. Or, if Maricar was doing an interview, they assumed that she already got the job. We stuck with the big picture to save ourselves from the highs and lows of their emotions.

I had to check myself often and follow my own advice. I'd find myself with my head in the clouds, thinking about life abroad. How would our day-to-day change? What new experiences would we have? Where would we go next? How would we change? These details were all shots in the dark, and spending my energy following the process was best.

The ideal scenario was securing a teaching position before we went on winter break so we could enjoy the holidays with our short-term future booked. That did not happen.

Even after applying to two dozen schools without an offer, Maricar came into the new year refreshed and motivated.

"All we need is one school to say yes, right? If that happened, it would set off a series of changes. I've got my first job fair this weekend in San Francisco."

"How does a job fair work?"

"Search Associates, a recruiting agency for international teaching jobs, said I should get there early with my resume and sign up to meet with interested schools. Those "meetings" are interviews with principals," she explained. "If they liked me, it was possible that they would provide me with an offer on the spot."

"Wow. They don't mess around."

"Slots fill up fast."

"How do you feel about it?"

"I am nervous because all I've gotten are a bunch of nos. However, I am confident in my abilities and experience, so if they pass on me, it's their loss."

"That's the spirit. Shall we go through more interview questions?"

"Hit me."

I pulled from a list of interview questions that Maricar had pre-selected. She was organized.

Maricar came back from the job fair early.

"What are your thoughts on Berlin? I interviewed with the principal, and he was 90% certain I got the job. He had one more interview later in the afternoon and he said he would get back to me tonight or at the latest tomorrow morning."

"Didn't we visit Berlin briefly over ten years ago during our mini-European holiday? I remember it being overcast the whole time and cold, but the beer was cheaper than water."

"Yep. That was Berlin."

"Should we start packing our bags?"

"Nothing is final yet, but it sounds like a good bet. Can you imagine living in Berlin?"

"It's in the middle of Europe which makes it a nice hub to visit the rest of the area by train or plane. I can't believe this is happening."

Nine p.m. rolled by.

"I haven't gotten anything back. Should I be concerned?"

"He said tonight or tomorrow morning, right? I'm sure he has a lot on his plate. Why don't you send him an email thanking him for his time, blah blah blah?"

"Okay."

Neither of us could sleep that night. We started making spreadsheets of action items in our heads while at the same time thinking that we didn't want to jinx it.

It wasn't until late afternoon the next day that Maricar heard back from the principal. He was short and direct, informing her that she didn't get the job.

Maricar and I read the email half a dozen times, fruitlessly trying to pull meaning. The email deflated us. Our hopes were crushed. We brushed it off, moved on to the next opportunity, and imagined life in another city, not Berlin.

"This one was close. Oh well, on to the next. Make sure you email back asking for feedback. Remember how you got your last teaching position from a referral that came from an initial no?"

All we needed was one yes. Maricar got so far in the process and had a principal with nothing but good things to say. This provided us with hope, and I knew if we stayed persistent, something would eventually pay off.

January turned into February without new leads, and I shifted my mental timeline to the following school year. These life changes take time, and we were not even three months in. I convinced myself this delay was for the better, allowing us to save money and better plan our time abroad. After all, we were well within the golden age of parenting window we've rallied around.

Then it happened.

Nearly one month after getting a no, Maricar received an email from the same Berlin principal, asking if she was still available and interested in a secondary math position. He explained that while they filled the original position she applied for, another one opened up, and it's hers if she wants it.

No additional interview was required. All she had to do was say yes. We jumped up and down with joy.

She played it cool via email and asked for the offer details before deciding.

The compensation was more than enough and not taxed. It was a bilingual school that all our kids could attend tuition free, which would help us greatly with the transition.

We discuss it to ensure we are confident and aligned with this path-altering decision.

"Why are we doing this again?"

"Any good reasons why we shouldn't do this?"

"Let's do it!"

With an official job offer, we share the news with the kids. We played out different scenarios and were ready for anything from disappointment to confusion to excitement. We told them what we knew. In the end, they were excited and bombarded us with questions.

"What about my stuffies?"

"What is going to happen to our house?"

"Where are we going to live?"

"When are we coming back?"

I imagine that they didn't know what this meant for them. It was as if we were going on a vacation where we would travel, sleep in new beds, and explore different activities each day via a tour guide. The big difference they couldn't wrap their head around was how long we would be away. This would be two years. But that's the challenge with time. We only start to better understand how to quantify it as more of it goes. At their age, everything blurred, and it was enough of a challenge to differentiate the days of the week and the seasons.

Like most things, we didn't have all the answers yet, but we reassured them that we'd figure it out together and would have a blast along the way.

Excitement about the path forward quickly gave way to a focus on execution, as we saw the next five months as our runway to the share the news and tackle endless logistics while life continued to unfold.

In Their Words:
We Are Moving

Jero (9):

- *I didn't know anything about Germany, but I was obsessed with Japan. I knew that they were allies during WWII. My friend Clarence said it was dangerous because there were Nazis.*

Lea (7):

- *I was excited to move because it was something new. Berlin sounded nice based on what Mommy said. The best part is that I heard there was going to be snow.*

Feris (4):

- *Feris doesn't remember this part of the adventure. At this time, she was settling into the Little Bridges preschool and socializing with all her new friends.*

6
WHEN DO WE GO PUBLIC?

February 2019

Were we overthinking this?

No. No. No. This was important. With a change this big, we needed to be consistent with our messaging and reassure everyone we knew what we were doing, even if we didn't. And remember, at the end of the day, they were asking questions because they loved us and wanted to support us. They just had our well-being in mind.

At least, this is what I told myself.

I anticipated a lot of why questions. We owed it to them and ourselves to ensure we thought through the details.

"Any second thoughts?"

"No. I'm sure about this."

Even if we haven't had these conversations in real life yet, we have been playing them out over the past few months in our heads, rationalizing our decisions.

The high-level overview was this:

"I'm excited to share that this fall, our family is moving to Berlin for two years. Maricar got a secondary math teaching position at the

John F. Kennedy School, an American-German international school. Jero, Lea, and Feris will enroll at the same school, and we will spend our weekends and holidays traveling all over Europe.

As the kids have graduated from diapers and are all school-aged, we wanted to provide and live this experience together before they grow up."

We anticipated three standard follow-up questions:

Question 1: "When did this all happen?"

Reading between the lines: "Are you sure you know what you are doing?"

Context: We had been holding our cards close to our chests, mainly because we didn't know until recently if this would happen. We had been thinking about this for a while, but it would feel out of left field for close friends and family. Naturally, our loved ones wanted to understand our decision. They wanted us to be sure we wanted it. Secondly, they want to know whether our planning would put us in the best position. The challenge was that the path we were switching from and switching to was unconventional. It might be difficult for others to comprehend.

Our response: "We have been thinking about this even before the kids were born. And over the years, the details fell into place once we decided to make it happen. We also gained the guts through the years, learning that we could actually pull this thing off. As for the timing, we are taking advantage of our limited golden age of parenting window. Feris just turned four, and middle school is only a few years away for Jero. We want to spend as much time with the kids and create as many memorable experiences as possible before they outgrow us. We still have a lot to figure out and have the potential to ruin our kids' lives, but we are sure about our intentions."

Question 2: "What's your timeline?"

Reading between the lines: "How much time do we have with you, and what happens next?"

Context: Once we decided on the high-level details and explained why we chose this for ourselves, most people brought it back to themselves, asking what it meant for our relationship moving forward. For these conversations, we focused on how we wanted to inform them as soon as we decided. We reminded them that the trip was finite and opened up the possibility of traveling together.

Our response: "Maricar just accepted the position recently. We are still processing this ourselves. However, we wanted to fill you in early. We aren't leaving until the summer, so even though there's a lot to do between now and then, we have plenty of time."

Question 3: "There must be a million things to get done. What can I do to help?"

Reading between the lines: "Can you fill me in on the juicy details?"

Context: Once the conversation got here, it was easy. It usually meant that someone accepted the initial news, started to get curious, and was ready to move forward with our relationship. Depending on the person, the conversation could flow in several directions, including downsizing plans, preparing for life abroad, or even combing through our growing checklist.

Our response: "Our initial plan was to take a year off and homeschool along the way, but we didn't win the lottery or were organized enough to think that far ahead. We were too busy with life. By using an international school as our home base, the transition will be a lot easier, and we can travel one step at a time without getting burned out. Our immediate step will be sending in our documents to the school who will take care of all our paperwork. Then, we will attempt to whittle down all our stuff into ten bags."

Moving Forward

With certainty that we were moving forward, we created a list of people, considered the conversations, and organized them by difficulty. For example, although filled with logistics, work conversations were the easiest because they were business.

On the other end of the spectrum were our parents, who had been in our corner since day one and had a personal stake in our long-term well-being. They wanted us to be happy and successful. The difficulty here was in our differing expectations of what that meant.

From their perspective, everything was perfect. We were living their dream. This was the life they imagined and wanted for their children. We were on the path that emphasized a good education, stable income, deep roots, and security. Changing a good thing didn't make sense.

I am one of three boys, and my parents would have my siblings and their families around. They were never in short supply of family. Maricar on the other hand, grew up primarily as an only child. With her father, Oscar, in the US Navy, it would often be only her and her mother, Esperanza. They had a strong bond, never being away from one another for more than a few months at a time.

When Jero was born, Esperanza dropped everything and moved in to be our children's primary caregiver. She was often the one who held the kids through the night and rocked them to sleep. The one that greeted them after school every day with a smile, a hug, and a snack. The one that would spoil them with sugar and screen time, taking the blame when Maricar or I figured out what was going on. In the process, she built a connection as if they were her own children. This was her sacrifice, a contribution to allow us to maintain a dual-income household and stay the course.

Logistically, her parents lived with us. This would mean that their purpose of raising their grandchildren and their definition of home was about to change. The news was heavy, and they took it hard despite our preparations.

They saw it as us separating as a family and took it as a personal attack, convincing themselves that we didn't want them to be a part of our lives. We anticipated this happening.

We focused the conversation on providing the kids with an international education and traveling the world. We showed them pictures of the school and reassured them that we knew what we were doing. This change was only temporary and meanwhile, we could plan a vacation together.

I don't think any of it helped. Whatever we said translated into the same message for them.

The next few months were awkward.

7

BOX, SELL, OR DONATE

May 2019

What should we do with all our stuff? Figuring this out and acting on it accounted for 80% of our headaches over the last three months.

By American standards, we had done a decent job getting rid of it over the years. Our youngest Feris was four, which meant we were past the toddler stage and all the accessories associated with the phase. We were 99% certain we were done expanding our family, so we enjoyed the purge of every dust-collecting and space-occupying item.

Yet even with our frequent culling, there seemed to be a never-ending well of things we hadn't touched in years.

For so long, we focused on accumulating stuff and filling our house with it. When we first moved in, our garage provided two parking spots. Over the years, stuff filled the space, and we could only park one car in the garage. Most recently, our garage became primarily a transition zone.

At first, letting go was hard. We attached meaning and significance to everything we had. And, if something were on its way out, someone would chime in with a reason we should keep it, whatever it was.

We sorted through the following:

- Random kitchen appliances
- Forgotten toys
- Brand new and unused clothes and shoes
- Barely used sports equipment
- Unopened gifts

This process would have been much more complicated if we had gone away for six months or a year. We knew we'd be right back in that time frame, and it would make sense to put stuff in storage. It would create a gray area of what is essential now and what we'd like to return to in one year. Fortunately, we didn't have this problem. We would bring what we needed, and when we came back, we would start with a clean slate. There wasn't much worth storing for two years that we couldn't acquire when we returned.

Occasionally, there was an item without any monetary value or practical use but carried sentimental meaning. There were two in particular that we sat on until we could come up with a solution. The first was a set of eight huge photo albums I started in high school and that extended to the present day. I digitized the pages and then tossed the physical albums. The second was a selection of baby clothes that all three kids used at one point. Maricar turned them into a quilt.

It was liberating to purge, and it got easier as our move date approached.

What was the transition plan? Over five months, we would go from living in our 2500 square-foot home to a temporary 1200 square-foot house for a month and then finally to a 350 square-foot room when we got to Berlin. Each person got two check-in bags and a personal carry-on.

We had to get down to ten bags. It was so small that we knew from the beginning that we could only keep the essentials like clothes, shoes, and school supplies. Everything else had to go. In a way, it made everything easier because it made the finish line concrete.

No, we didn't want to pay extra to ship anything in advance or get additional check-in bags.

No, we didn't want to pay for storage.

Yes, we had family we could leave stuff with, but we didn't want to burden them.

We knew there would be a scramble in the last few weeks, regardless of what we did. Therefore, we saw every item discarded, regardless of how small, as a step in the right direction.

"These towels and plates are still in their original packaging, a gift from our wedding over ten years ago. We are never going to use it right?" I asked.

"Right. Don't show it to my mom. She tries to intercept everything we are trying to donate." Maricar mentioned.

"It's like whatever we donate comes right back in."

Not only was this all a transition for us, but it was also a transition for my in-laws. We had to balance our urgency to move forward while being sensitive to their needs and resistance to change.

"What are your parents going to do with all of their stuff?"

"Same thing they do all the time. Send it to the Philippines, bring it with them, or now, put it in storage."

This was stressing me out just thinking about it.

Maricar's parents had strong emotional ties to their possessions, which were deeply intertwined with their sense of identity. This made it difficult to broach the topic without it becoming another personal attack. We decided to let them come to their own conclusions about how to manage their belongings, as we had our own issues to address. By giving them space, we hoped they would find a solution that aligned with their values and needs. To make this transition more complicated, life didn't stop.

While downsizing, we approached the last six months with a new sense of urgency for spending time with friends and family and doing all the Bay Area activities we could squeeze in. This also meant that we still needed some stuff. I shed a small tear every time we needed something I had just donated.

"Can I use the pump for my basketball?"

"Did I already sell my biking shoes?"

"I haven't used my wetsuit in three years, and now someone invites me for an open water swim?"

"Do we still have my soccer stuff?"

Where did all our stuff end up? There were four major channels we used:

Craigslist: This had been my default second-hand market for many years, and it had not changed much except for losing its once-dominant position. We got rid of some big-ticket items here, but it seemed too much work for anything else. The clunky platform didn't provide identification verification or communication features that have become standard on apps.

Savers: This was a thrift store, and we had one ten minutes from home. It was conveniently located, so I would pass it on my daily commute. There was also a Goodwill, but the great thing about Savers was their supported drive-through donation station. I would queue up for all of one minute, and then when it was my turn, I'd toss my bags of stuff into their bins. When I timed it right, I could be in and out of this place in less than three minutes. I was here multiple times a week, offloading our clothes, bedding, toys, small appliances, and furniture.

Friends and family: Most people already had enough stuff. However, there were instances of family and friends picking up a new sport, moving into a new place, or having younger kids. This was a great win-win channel because we felt our stuff was going to a good place.

Facebook Marketplace: This was the evolution that Craigslist did not make. While selling a laundry list of items here, there were several features I came to appreciate:

Mobile first: The experience was designed to be mobile-friendly, so I never had to go to a desktop.

Seamless posting options: The ability to add a picture and description quickly was helpful for multiple items.

Standard communication tools within the app: There wasn't a dance between texting, calls, and emails.

Location Tools: With the cost of gas being so high, buyers were doing the math. *Free isn't really free if I have to spend $10 on gas and my time, right?*

Profile: When dealing with the second-hand market, you don't know much about the person you are doing business with. However, having a profile helped hold people accountable and provided a level of professionalism. There were significantly fewer no-shows.

And then, there was the big stuff we had to time out.

The goal was to use the essential big-ticket items until the last minute, all while having enough wiggle room that we didn't get stuck with them or, at worst, we have to pay to get rid of them.

Even in a major metro like the Bay Area, you need a car, especially in the suburbs. We had places and things to do, so we needed a car until the last minute. We also recognize that you don't sell cars overnight.

Our cars were reliable Hondas, paid off, and in good condition. If all else failed, we could drive to CarMax and sell them in an hour, but we would get half of what was possible on the private market. The extra money would be helpful.

After selling and buying countless items on Craigslist over the years, I learned to filter out those who liked to kick the tires. You know the type. They get your hopes up, ask a million questions, waste your time, and, more often than not, don't buy.

I was patient and found a buyer for the Honda Odyssey. I sold it a month before we left. As a temporary replacement, my parents had a comparable car we could use. It was a lifesaver.

Unlike other transactions, I have never had to hold on to this much cash. The person who bought the Odyssey handed me a large stack of hundreds wrapped in a rubber band. I felt exposed.

I sold the Honda Accord two weeks before we left, giving us only one car to share. I then became dependent on my bike.

And what about the other big-ticket item, our house?

This could have been an enormous pain, but we took steps to make it easy.

We considered listing it as a short-term rental but quickly scrapped that idea because of our location in the suburbs. The only people who wanted to hang out in San Ramon were the people who lived there. We decided to rent it out. Plenty of families in the market dreamed of living in front of a pristine park and sending their kids to award-winning schools.

A property manager, Ben, helped handle all the details and headaches.

The hard part was deciding when the property would be available and securing temporary housing until we flew out.

The first priority was finding the best tenant. This meant we had to provide a sooner start date to keep our options for prospective tenants open. Our target was a family who wanted to move in during the summer to settle in, enroll in the local schools, and be ready for the fall classes. And, if we were moving into the neighborhood, we'd want to have as much lead-up time to the start of school to settle in.

Unfortunately, this overlapped with our other timeline of staying in our house until we left for Berlin. We cut it close.

"James, we have an interested renter who checks all the boxes. The catch is that they would like to move in a week earlier."

"That would mean we'd have to move out the week after school ends. That's cutting it close, Ben."

"Well, it would actually have to be sooner. You need to move out all your stuff so that I can have the place cleaned and inspected for the expected ready date. That would mean by Sunday."

"The last day of school is on Friday, so we'd have only a day or so to make the transition. This should be fun. I'll speak with Maricar to figure out if and how we can pull this off."

Thirty-six hours after the kids left school, we had to leave our once-upon-a-time forever house. We had plenty of time leading up to the last day, and if carefully planned, it would be stress-free. It wasn't, but it worked to our advantage in the grander scheme of things. My younger brother, Jeff, conveniently had a house in San Leandro, about 20 miles away, that was vacant for the month or so before our flight. This house gave us a place to move to and served as a transition area.

It forced us to sort through our things. We thought we had cut down to the essentials, but when moving stuff from one house to the next, we realized how much we still needed to deal with.

The house was more like an apartment and less than half the square footage we were used to living in. And in just four weeks, we would move to a space that's a third of this one. This helped us adjust to close living quarters. As a silver lining, we were close to the Oakland Airport which was only five miles away. If we couldn't get a ride, we were now close enough to run there.

And what about my in-laws during this time? They were with us for every part of the move, going through the transitions until we left for Berlin. Their resistance to change made it hard until they learned to embrace it and find their own opportunity. They retired, bought a house, and were preparing to live two lives: one in the US and the other in the Philippines, taking advantage of both worlds.

With the exception of our dining table set, we hadn't invested much in furniture over the years. It looked like the assortment that a college student would cobble together on a budget. We liked the idea of coming back to a clean slate. Upon return, it would give us a fresh start for the next phase of our life.

Despite a mixed bag of furniture, each served a purpose, and for every item we sold or donated, we had to adjust. For the last three weeks, we sat on foldable chairs, boxes, or step stools. We slept on the floor or on an uncomfortable inflatable mattress with a slow leak.

Jero said, "I miss my own room and bed. How much longer do we have to do this?"

"Three weeks, but it's not going to get any easier in Germany. Think of it as character-building."

"Character building . . . what's that?"

"Forget about it. You'll find out."

We started having these conversations and change experiences early. I didn't know what to expect when we moved to Germany, but I knew we would have to adapt and embrace change. A lot of change.

I also knew that we would need to rely on one another to help us process everything that was changing around us.

Lastly, I knew that the kids would look to Maricar and me for guidance in everything. To get through these stressful times, we reminded ourselves about the larger why and that it was our choice. This worked to get us to the next checkpoint.

What did we learn?

When we assessed everything, we got a reality check on how much we had. It became more obvious when we tried to move it around and learned how many trips it would take. In the end, we let go of nearly everything because it was all just stuff.

The value we placed on stuff was greatly inflated; it was worth significantly much less. For us, it held a story and memories, making it far more valuable than its worth to others.

As our move date approached, we accepted reality and willingly gave it away. It felt good. In the moment, it might have been hard to let go, but not even a day later, we forgot all about it.

Over the years, we saved many items for "just in case" but never used them. Examples included clothing with tags on them, extra kitchen dishes or random appliances, and bath towels. Even our pantry was full of untouched spices or goods.

We did it. Everything fit into our ten 70-liter duffel bags. If we missed anything, we had a Mastercard.

Moving forced us to reevaluate our relationship with possessions. With limited space, accumulating more would only weigh us down. For the life and path we were embarking on, mobility and freedom from encumbrances were essential. But this shift raised new questions: What other challenges lie ahead? How would our day-to-day lifestyle transform?

In Their Words:
Pack It Up

Jero (9):

- *I was taking iron drops at the time. It was terrible and gross with a metallic taste. I hid it in the closet so we would leave it behind.*
- *I packed the game console, and my dad asked, "What are you doing? We aren't going to have a TV."*
- *On the drive to the airport, Papa Joker gave me some random stuff from his van, including a phone charger. I didn't even have a phone.*
- *My grandparents dropped us off, and we watched them get further away as we went up the escalator. I almost cried but was also excited, so I didn't.*

Lea (7):

- *Every single spring, Mommy would make us donate all our toys, so I don't think we had too much to get rid of.* [Note from James: Every year was an event. We'd go into the toy room and dump out all the contents on the floor, and then there was a sorting process. The kids weren't happy about it, but they gave in.]
- *When it came to packing up, I thought I could bring all my*

remaining toys to Berlin, so I put them all in a box. What I wasn't told was it was being put into storage at my grandparents' house.

- *About a month before leaving, we moved to San Leandro (Uncle Jeff's old house), to be near the airport. Filled these big blue bags with all our stuff.*

Feris (4)

- *Feris doesn't remember this part of the adventure. Her interests at this time were reading Bob Books, riding her balance bike, and following Lea around.*

8
CAN I CHANGE MY ANSWER?

July 2019

Today was the day. We would leave for Berlin later this afternoon, and although I only got a few hours of sleep because of last-minute packing, I needed to get my morning run in.

The streets were quiet. I had them to myself, giving me time to express my thoughts.

When did this idea of living a life of adventure even come about?

Was it the result of one too many viewings of Pixar's *Up*? Do we see ourselves as Carl? Were we just septuagenarians going on an adventure in a flying house to search for our dream destination before we bite the dust?

Adventure is out there!

Could we still back out? Would we be able to return things to how they were . . . back to our normal?

Not that long ago, I thought we already had life figured out.

Growing up, I was instilled with a blueprint, a path on how to make it in life: get good grades, attend a good university, get a job, get married, earn a few promotions, buy a house, have kids, and don't deviate from the plan. That was the American Dream. A belief passed down that if you paid your dues, you were guaranteed financial security, success, and happiness. But was it guaranteed?

Our boxes were checked. We were on track, doing all of the above, and by some accounts, ahead of the game. Nothing was broken.

Why did we have to rock the boat? Why did I have ideas of grandeur?

The sacrifices we had made, our parents had made, and the support we had gotten from friends and family over the years to get here were countless.

Did I want to give all that up so we could pretend to live in some travel magazine? Have a few precious moments?

If someone proposed this idea at work, I wouldn't take the bait. I'd take a step back and ask myself, *what's the problem you are trying to solve? Why is your current life a problem?*

Sometimes, we get so caught up in the solution and the execution that we forget to ask the right questions. The truth that many people can't handle is that not all problems are worthy of our limited attention. Sometimes, it's best to ignore that itch, tangent, that distraction so we can focus our time and resources on things that matter. Is this one of those problems?

What am I doing?

Am I just overthinking all this?

Am I just having cold feet?

For years, my gut has been telling me that something wasn't right.

But in the past few months, we had made the decision and completed our homework. Now, we needed to trust the process and see where it will take us. We flipped the script and were on a new path—one unique to us—a journey that would change our surroundings and reset our expectations, allowing us to spend more time together and create memorable experiences.

As I finished my route, I started thinking, "we got this." I felt refreshed, ready for whatever was next.

A few hours later, our parents dropped us off at the airport. It felt like the first day of school. The airport check-in process was quick, and the next thing we knew, we were going through security and saying goodbye. There were tears.

Goodbyes are often easier for those who are leaving. Our sadness was outshone by our excitement to start a new life chapter together. One that we had chosen by design. As far as we were concerned, we were ready.

Or so we thought.

PART TWO
OUR JOURNEY UNSCRIPTED

As we adventured, we had much to learn about navigating our expectations and realities while moving and traveling abroad during a world-changing pandemic.

9

GOT A EURO?

Berlin, July 2019 (Week 0)

1, 2, 3, 4, 5, 6, 7, 8, 9, 10. That's all of them.

When they checked us in back in Oakland, the service counter staff seemed like he was multitasking, putting me in doubt of his focus the whole time. After a layover and an entire day of travel, I was certain we'd lose at least one bag by the time we arrived in Germany. I was only hoping it was the one with our extra shoes and school supplies, items we could easily replace.

Each bag was bigger and heavier than Jero. The other two didn't stand a chance. Rather than attempting to move the bags, Lea and Feris were already getting comfortable. I couldn't blame them since our internal clocks were confused by the nine-hour time difference.

We had made it. I'm pumped with adrenaline and soaked in the terminal's surroundings. This airport was more dated than the one back home.

Okay. First task: secure a trolley, or else we wouldn't get anywhere. Easy enough.

"Does anyone see the trolleys?"

"The *what*?"

"A trolley for our bags."

I assumed they were all tired and ready to fall asleep if given someplace to lie down. I tried to keep everyone engaged before they got too comfortable.

"There they are. I'll grab one."

Jero came back with a look of confusion and no trolley.

"What happened?"

"They are locked together, and there is a coin slot. I think we need to pay for them."

All I had were US dollar bills, and no change machine was in sight.

"Daddy, I think that's an information booth. Maybe they have change."

I loved Jero's willingness to help.

"Good idea."

I walked over to the booth and spoke to the information receptionist. In my gentle, but pleading English, I asked, "Where do I get a coin for the trolley?"

He responded with what sounded like shouting in German. I didn't understand.

I tried again, a bit slower, and still in English. He responded in German, with what I assume is the same thing he said earlier and again in a tone that feels like shouting. This back-and-forth wasn't going anywhere. My face was turning red.

I did my best impression of pushing a trolley and inserting a coin. He then pointed out the stacked trolleys I'm already familiar with. After five frustrating minutes of trying to ask for a coin, I gave up and walked away.

That didn't work.

"I'm thirsty. Can I get a Coke?" asks Lea.

"No. It's full of sugar, and the caffeine isn't going to do you any favors."

Maricar chimed in, "You should buy a Coke. I have a few euros that my aunt gave me."

"Why? Are you thirsty?"

"Not really, but you'll get change."

Getting a trolley was a family effort, and we were lost for ten minutes.

I learned later that everyone carries a euro coin with them. Some European wallets even have a slot specifically for this one reusable coin. After learning this information, I never left home without a euro stashed in my pocket and even an emergency backup in my bag.

We loaded our trolley and in no time our chaperone, sent by the school, greeted us, and took us to our apartment to settle in.

There was no corporate housing, so we had to find an apartment before arriving. We needed a space large enough to accommodate our family of five, fit within our limited budget, and be close to the school around which our lives would revolve. We did not want to commute, so location was everything. We settled on Zehlendorf, a leafy suburb, not the gritty urban landscape that people might associate with Berlin.

Most places were a no. However, we found a unique situation where a young family of five bilingual Germans had planned a seven-month sabbatical in Australia from October through April. They planned to rent out their fully furnished apartment while they were away.

The problem is that we needed a place upon arrival in July.

We worked out a deal where we would live in their basement bedroom at a significantly reduced rate for the first two months and then take over the entire apartment when they left. When they returned from their sabbatical, we would find another apartment—a win-win.

Let's start with our big reservation about the situation. We would all be living in one room and sharing a bathroom. To clarify, this was not a one-bedroom apartment. It was a bedroom with a bathroom. It would be a giant leap from our four-bed, two-and-a-half-bath situation where everyone had their own space and plenty to spare.

On the other hand, given our temporary and mobile situation, we saw numerous benefits that had us jump on the offer.

The first was that we'd have a place to stay upon arrival, and if it didn't work out, we wouldn't have a long-term contract locking us down. With all the plates we were juggling with our move, this provided much-needed peace of mind.

We saw living with an English-German-speaking landlord as a bonus. She could help us with all our cultural questions and paperwork. At the time, we didn't know how valuable and important this lifeline would be.

It was move-in ready and perfect for our short-term needs. We didn't have to worry about furniture or accumulating stuff because we didn't have the space and the landlord would provide everything we needed. Utilities were also included. This was wonderful as we heard horror stories about the internet taking months to install.

Lastly, this plan would save us money we could use for travel. Now, because we only had one income, this financial cushion was helpful.

We had to get through the first few months, and everything would work out. And like I told the kids; this whole experience would build character. Looking back at our reasons, we were desperate to check the housing box, finding ways to convince ourselves it was a good decision.

When we arrived at the apartment, our landlord greeted us and showed us to our room. There were no surprises, but with all our stuff and everyone present simultaneously, it felt claustrophobic. There wasn't enough room to move, let alone sit down. How are we going to manage to sleep? We'd cross that bridge soon enough.

It was either the room or my excitement, but I was ready to get out and explore our new surroundings. There was a new-teacher event for families at a *Biergarten*, a beer garden, and this would be the perfect way to start our German adventure. Maricar wisely put me in check.

"There will be other Biergartens. The kids are tired and hungry, and we have a big first week ahead of us to get ready for the first day of school. "

We did the practical thing. We found something to eat from our welcome basket, cleaned up, and figured out sleeping arrangements. Three shared the bed and two found space to lay out the floor mats. It was Tetris.

It's obvious now, but I should have realized that two things would be happening a lot over the next few days, weeks, and months.

1. We would be looking lost a lot.
2. We would get "put into place" a lot.

It was baptism by fire, and we learned quickly in the first few days. Everyone in the community saw it as their responsibility to uphold the rules, and they weren't shy about holding us accountable.

We had this experience a lot, especially at the grocery store and in bike lanes.

"Ding! Ding! Ding!" followed by shouting in German.

I jumped as I tried to get out of the way, unsure which direction to move. On this walk alone, this happened to us three times. New to Berlin, I wasn't sure if it was shouting or just a firm authoritative tone. Regardless, the effect was the same on my ego.

I placed my hands on my head, half because of shame and half out of confusion.

"What did he say? What are we getting called out for now?"

We all stared at one another with puzzled looks. It was all so fast that I didn't have time to pull out Google Translate.

We ran through the possible offenses:

Were we biking in the wrong lane? Wrong direction? Going too slow? We weren't even on a bike, so it can't be any of those.

I asked the kids, "Were any of you walking in the bike lane?"

"What bike lane?"

We all look down and can see some faded lines.

We were walking in the bike lane. We learned to watch for it, although sometimes, it would be hard to see.

Our kids were used to learning new rules and adjusting, so they didn't take any criticism or instruction personally. As an adult, however, I felt anxious and guarded every time. Usually, the issue was a lack of consideration for others, which was perceived as offensive.

Were we taking too long to bag our groceries?

Were we mindlessly standing and blocking the aisle?

Were we speaking above a whisper?

In the first month, I swear I got reprimanded in the grocery store more than my twelve years at Catholic School and Sundays at church.

I learned to leave the kids at home and have them wait outside or get in and out as quickly as possible if I had to bring them. These measures were to minimize the number of things I could get scolded for.

When was the last time you were scolded as an adult? It doesn't happen often, especially by a stranger. I felt like a little boy all over again. I was always on edge.

And, to make matters worse, I couldn't communicate back. Even with the little German I knew, I would freeze up, stutter, and my words would come out jumbled.

With six months of preparation, you would think we'd spend more time learning the language before arriving. A dozen other priorities and the experience points we earned through Duolingo from individual lessons and practice proved worthless in reality.

My go-to phrases were:

"*Es tut mir Leid. Ich spreche kein Deutsch*. I'm sorry. I don't speak German."

Or for short, "Entschuldigung. Englisch?"

In return, I'd get a disappointed look, head-shaking, and more German. Using everything but the words coming out of their mouth, I'd figure out what they were trying to tell me.

Now and then, someone would feel sorry for me and start to tell me what I did wrong in English so I could correct it the next time.

Beyond the day-to-day of learning German grocery norms and figuring out how to get from one place to the next, there was a laundry list of things to get done that we had to work through as

Maricar was gearing up for her first time teaching high-school-aged students in an international bilingual school.

That's a handful to say and a lot of big-time firsts we had on our plates:

- Wellness checks
- Bank accounts
- Cell phone plans
- School supplies
- After school care
- Meal plans
- Bicycles and helmets
- Health benefits

On paper, these were basic errands on anyone's list. Still, because we were doing this internationally with language barriers and encountering unexpected obstacles, every accomplishment was a huge win. It had to be because, in this situation, there were more failures than wins. I didn't give the kids enough credit at the time, but they got into a positive rhythm, knowing that we had to get something done each day and take it one step at a time.

Like most of the things that were happening, the kids were curious about what was going on.

"What are we doing today?"

"A wellness check. It doesn't look far, so we can just walk."

"How long is it going to take?"

"Hopefully just an hour."

"Can we take the bus?"

"We can, but I'm still not sure which one to take. I don't want to get us lost again."

"What's a wellness check?"

"It's just to make sure you are fit to be in school."

"Will there be needles?"

"I hope not."

The kids had so many questions, and after they became tired of hearing, "I don't know," I began making up answers to give them confidence that I knew what I was doing.

We were in it together, sharing our mistakes and passing on newly learned cultural norms. Everything was a first, and despite the embarrassment and shame we would feel after someone yelled at us or the confused helplessness we would experience, we could always confide in one another for support.

The dinner table—or rather, a work desk converted into an eating space—became our gathering centerpiece. Beyond the first meal, when jet lag dominated, silence was scarce. Someone always had a tale to share, and, fueled by constant togetherness, each person would build upon the story, creating a snowball effect.

As we embarked on each new day, wonder and curiosity filled our minds. Our journey was marked by countless ups and downs, twists and turns. Far from glamorous, these shared moments became the most vivid and unforgettable memories of our adventure.

In Their Words:
First Impressions of Berlin

Jero (9):

- *We got picked up in a big van, and they gave us sparkling water, fruit, and crackers. I was relieved because I was so hungry. The last time we ate was on the plane.*
- *I had a jacket, thinking it was going to be cold, but there was a heat wave going on. It was muggy with gray skies.*
- *On the day we arrived, I was okay because excitement kept me going. I remember waking up at 3 a.m., and I was so tired. We went to visit "L'DL." It wasn't an apostrophe. It was the top of an "i." It's actually LiDL. We didn't know there were different types of water and accidentally bought the sparkling water. No one liked it. To drink it, we would shake it to get the fizz out.*

Lea (7):

- *I remember when we first got into our apartment, we set up our purple mattresses on the floor and then went upstairs to play with the other kids. I couldn't sleep that night, so I stayed up and stared out the window. I was really tired the next day.*
- *For our first full day, we did a lot of stuff. We walked down the hill to go to a cafe. Sat with a girl and her dad. I think my dad*

knew them. We really didn't order anything, and then we went to the school and the teachers' lounge.

- *The school looked really big. It went from kindergarten through high school. It was pretty clean. I liked the playground because it had a huge pyramid. I remember being the fastest person in my class to get to the top. I had a technique. I fell off once and landed on my back.*

Feris (4):

- *Feris doesn't remember this part of the adventure. She was enrolled in kindergarten and participated in the Einschulung, school enrollment, ceremony. Feris had her own Schultüte, or "school cone," a decorated cardboard cone of gifts.*
- *She distinguished her friends as English or German-speaking and loved reading every Dr. Seuss book she could find.*

10
TRAIN TO PRAGUE

Prague, September 2019 (Week 6)

It was the Friday before a three-day weekend, and I had an open WhatsApp line with Maricar. There was the potential of leaving early, so I'm messaging her to see if she had any real-time news from her colleagues.

"What's happening over there? Any updates?"

"How about now?"

No response. I waited anxiously.

The morning weather report called for record high temperatures, which for Berlin schools, meant there was a chance of *Hitzefrei*. *Hitzefrei* translates to "heat-free." The law states that if there is excessive heat, students and employees can take the rest of the day off.

With so much happening, from settling into our apartment, learning German customs, back-to-school shopping, and filling endless amounts of paperwork—thank God for Google Translate—the American Labor Day weekend snuck up on us. Yes, at the John F. Kennedy Schule, a German and American school, we celebrated the holidays of both countries.

It was 11 a.m., and still, no response. The school would make announcements before lunch, so any time now. With the possibility of the long weekend starting earlier, the teachers were even more excited than their students. I refreshed my phone, thinking it would make a difference.

A text came in.

"School canceled. Be home soon."

I quickly shifted into go mode, putting the final touches on packing and closing down the apartment so that we would be ready to leave when everyone arrived. I had a few minutes before I needed to pick up Feris, so I took a moment to process the whirlwind of the last few weeks. My priority was ensuring everyone felt comfortable and supported in their new setting and that box had been checked. The last thing on my mind was traveling, but here we were, about to dip our toe outside Berlin.

I snapped out of my daydream and arrived at school in time to pick up Feris. I strapped her to the backseat of the bike and waved at Jero and Lea, letting them know it was a race home. Jero took a shortcut through the park and was already locking up his bike when I arrived.

These few extra hours were a godsend and would provide a buffer to catch our five-hour train to Prague. On paper, it seemed simple enough, but as we had learned already, nothing was easy.

The kids were giddy with anticipation, and it wasn't because of Prague. They didn't even know where it was. We planned to take a long-distance train and travel with two other American families we had met. Having their friends around made all the difference.

After two train transfers, we arrived at the Berlin Hauptbahnhof twenty minutes early. It was massive and more like a multilevel mall. We scanned a map and learned trains were on the top and bottom floors, and then there were stores and restaurants of every kind sandwiched between. We descended the escalators, eyeing potential snacks as we made our way to the bottom floor. Our train would be arriving in ten minutes. It was stressful, but we couldn't have timed it better. I felt I should pat myself on the back whenever we arrived on time.

My stomach grumbled.

I asked Maricar, "I saw an *Edeka* [the largest supermarket chain in Germany] with a bakery only one flight up. Do I have enough time to grab a snack, or should I stay here to make sure we have enough time to get on the right train?"

I didn't give her a chance to respond.

I walked off with my growling stomach, got a *Laugenbroetchen*, a pretzel bun, and returned just as the train slowed down.

"Perfect timing as usual," I smiled. Maricar rolled her eyes.

Our train approached.

"I think this one is ours."

The kids were in their own world, and I told them to grab their bags because it was time to get on the train.

As soon as the train came to a complete stop, the other passengers immediately and expertly boarded at their assigned cabin, put their stuff away, and sat down.

In less than a minute, the platform was empty, and we were the only ones running along the platform. The conductor blew his whistle.

"Already? The train just got here."

In a panic, we all jumped into the nearest train wagon.

"Did everyone get on?"

I took a quick look out the window, and I didn't see anyone from our group standing on the platform. Good so far.

I texted Maricar.

"You on? Do you have Jero and Feris?"

"Yes."

"Got Lea?"

"Yes."

Our trip could have ended on that platform, and it would have been a horrible weekend.

We learned our first lesson of the week. Before the train arrives, use the platform markings to line up in front of your assigned car. If you don't have an assigned seat, there is a designated "first come, first serve" section. Once the train arrives, there is no time to walk the platform. You just get on before it leaves you behind.

Now we know, and knowing was half the battle.

It was time to find our seats. With our luggage, we squeezed through passengers to get to the other side of the train, saying our most common German word these days—*entschuldigung*, excuse me.

"Where are our seats?"

"It's first come, first serve so we need to find open seats."

"How about these?"

"This area is first class and has reserved seats. We need to get on the second-class train. Once we get there, we can take any seat."

We made it to the second-class train, and—surprise! —no seats remained. We desperately and hopelessly roamed the aisles after each stop, waiting for people to get off, but there was no change.

Then, the questions came pouring in.

"Daddy, where are our seats? How long do we need to stand? I'm tired."

"Why didn't we just get reserved seats?"

"Good questions."

I didn't have any good answers. *What was I thinking?* A Friday afternoon train leaving Berlin—of course, there would be no seats.

Rewind to when I purchased our tickets. I had the option of buying reserved first-class seats at a marginal difference, but I thought everyone on the train still gets to the same place. Why pay more? If given the chance again, I would gladly pay the small difference.

We spent most of the five-hour ride standing separately or sitting on the aisle floor when our legs gave out. Not fun. Before entering the Czech Republic, the train had a mass exodus in Dresden and we took advantage, finally finding seats.

There were better ways to start the first part of our trip on a Friday afternoon.

"Should I get *korunas* [the currency of the Czech Republic]?"

"The Czech Republic is part of the EU so most places should accept Euros or a card."

"Maybe just enough for the tram then. We should be able to pay for everything with a card. The last thing we want is to be stuck with a pocket full of korunas."

I conservatively withdrew money from the ATM. This would bite me later.

We checked into our shared Airbnb late that night, and the following day, we did all the touristy things in the city center. On our second day, we decided to explore on bikes and ended up at a local farmers' market with food and treats we had to have. They only accepted cash, and the kids were hangry after the ride to get there.

"Daddy, can you just get some money? Why didn't you bring more? Use your credit card."

I searched for the nearest ATM. A notorious blue and gold Euronet machine was conveniently positioned right next to the market. If you look them up online, every travel website will tell you the same message: Avoid these machines at all costs.

Why? They are strategically placed so that people who need cash have no other option. The machine charges a convenience tax in three ways: 1) Just using the machine will charge you a transaction fee; 2) An unfavorable exchange rate will give you cents for every dollar; and 3) You will face a misleading conversion fee.

I was their target demographic: an unprepared traveler in need of cash. I paced back and forth a few times in front of the machine, believing an alternative option would present itself. Nope. I felt the pressure to deliver, and I got the cash and plenty of it.

We quickly went from a famine to feast mentality. Instead of not having any money, we now had an overabundance that we had to use before we left. The beef sliders, chimney cake filled with ice cream, and random pastries were amazing. I was a hero.

Prague gave us a handful of unique experiences.

Rubbing raw garlic on fried toast and then topping it with beef tartare was good to try once but never again. Maybe I did it wrong, but it tasted like I was biting directly into the garlic, and my breath was on fire for the rest of the day.

Did you know that beer there comes in three-gallon jugs? It comes in *světlý ležák*, a light lager, or *tmavý ležák*, a dark lager. They kept things simple and in high supply—a significant change from my craft beer preference.

We took a tandem bike ride along the river and then rode the shortest "river cruise" from one bank to the other. I had never seen anything like it: a small barge that would travel all of a few meters to take people to the other side. I wondered whether the skipper got bored. At what point would it make more sense to build a bridge?

We rode a funicular, an elevator that moves diagonally, and would become familiar with these on future European trips. It was the most foreign contraption and blew my mind.

We were only a short distance away in the Czech Republic, yet a world of difference in food, people, and culture. If we were back in the States, we would have spent the weekend at a backyard BBQ and, if we were lucky, a pool. That wouldn't have been a bad thing, but out here, even the tiniest excursions or trips could become a core memory. And even if things didn't go right, which was often the case, it was a lesson we would bank for future trips.

The train ride back was much easier. We splurged and upgraded our seats to first class for 5% more.

"This was so much fun. When can we do this again?"

"Just you wait. This is a teaser. You haven't seen anything yet."

They could have grumbled about standing for most of the train ride or walking in the heat, and maybe, in the moment, they did. But when the trip ended, they cherished the good stuff–the breathtaking views from our Airbnb, the multiple daily ice cream trips, and strolling with their friends at the Spiderman bridge. I was thrilled that the kids had fun.

Through adventures like these, we were shaping our family culture, one that prizes curiosity, open-mindedness to new experiences and a willingness to learn from mistakes.

In Their Words:
Prague

Jero (9):

- *This was our first trip outside of Germany, and I remembered being at the Yoshi's planning it. I was disappointed because I thought we would ride an ICE* [InterCity Express] train, *which looked really fancy and fast.*
- *I remember being confused when we first got on the train and had to use random seats until we found a cabin reserved for families. I was envious of the Steeles, who had nice seats in first class.*
- *We visited the John Lennon wall, and that's when I learned that we share the same birthday.*
- *The funnel cakes we had with ice cream and covered in sugar tasted a bit like Cinnabon.*

Lea (7):

- *I think this is the place with the big bridge where they filmed a part of* Spiderman. *It had a lot of faces on it and was supposedly historical. We saw a lot of old stone buildings and naked statues.*

- *We stayed with the Yoshis and Steeles in an Airbnb. These were two other families that we met in Europe. I learned that my friend, Elizabeth, brushed her teeth after she eats breakfast instead of before. I thought that was weird, but I gave it a try. I brushed my teeth after I ate, and she brushed her teeth before.*

Feris (4):

- *I remember the blue monkey statue with the shiny golden blob between his legs.*

11
WE HAVE NOTHING TO WORRY ABOUT

Napoli, February 2020 (Week 27)

"Why Napoli?"

"Skyscanner says that tickets are cheap."

"I don't even know where that is or what there is to do there."

"It's in Italy, the birthplace of pizza. We'll figure out the rest. And, if you have a better idea, I'm all ears. If not, let's go."

It was like spinning the bottle, figuring out where we'd go next. With a limited window of two years in Europe, you would think we would be more strategic and work from a bucket list. Nope.

Personally, I didn't care where we went. If we went somewhere new and were together, we'd find a way to make magic happen. It didn't take much. And because we were getting tickets on Skyscanner and traveling during the off-season, we were getting a bargain.

Growing up in California, I only knew one season. The "off-season" wasn't in my vocabulary.

By this time, we were six months into this adventure, comfortable with our routines, and a handful of trips under our belt, including two weeks in Spain, a road trip to Austria, every

Weihnachtsmarkt, Christmas market, we could find, and even a visit to Neuschwanstein Castle, the inspiration to Disney's Cinderella castle. During Christmas and Silvester (Germany's New Year) we had a handful of visitors: friends from UCLA and Maricar's parents. The visits, especially from Maricar's parents, helped us to reconnect with the familiar and reassure them all was good.

A week of school stood between us and our *Winterferien*, winter break.

Feris and I inspected the frost buildup on the bike seat. I pulled a rag from my backpack to wipe off the water droplets but realized they were frozen. I put more muscle into it to scrape off the layer of ice. I've learned that if I didn't go through this process, Feris would spend the first half of the day with wet pants. No one likes a wet bottom.

"Feris, does the seat look good?"

She inspects. "You missed a spot."

"How about now?"

"Okay."

In one swift motion, I balanced the bike with one hand while I loaded her carefully with the other. I buckled her in, crept out the gate looking both ways, and entered the bike lane.

Jero and Lea were already on their way to school.

It was the middle of winter, so shrubs that line the bike lane have been given a trim and have gone dormant. I didn't have to worry about a whack from an overgrown branch. There were still the loose bricks, cars that appeared out of nowhere, and impatient bikers that dangerously passed.

The school rush hour happened at 7:50 a.m., and everyone was trying to beat the bell. We fell in line with the rest of the bikers heading down Mühlenstraße. Germans learn to ride early, and we saw a kid who couldn't be older than four trying to keep up. Ahead of us was a front-loaded cargo bike with two kids in the passenger seat. Electric bikes zoomed past. They scared me because you could never hear them coming, and then they just whizzed by.

I was hyperaware of accidents waiting to happen because of my precious cargo. With Feris in the back, I took turns wide and slowly. I dropped her once, and I'm not proud of it. Thankfully, she forgave me and has forgotten all about it.

We arrived at the school, and I did everything in reverse. I took off Feris's belt, balanced the bike, placed her down, and removed her helmet before sending her off.

It wasn't raining, and I crossed my fingers, hoping the sun might peek through the clouds at some point today. That was considered good weather for a Berlin winter. Fellow kindergarten parents loitered around for small talk in their puffy jackets. The gossip this morning? COVID.

"What's the news?"

"Did you know that Italy is closing its northern borders? We were planning on driving there and enjoying an eco-friendly stay on a farm. That's now all questionable with how things are escalating."

Another parent decided to scrap their trip to Portugal in favor of a local trip to the Alps.

I nodded and attempted to put on a face of contemplation.

At the time, I thought that people were overreacting. It was the media at it again, over-sensationalizing a disease and making news out of nothing. Like everything else, this would blow over in a few weeks, and when we returned from holiday, the talk would be about what Trump said, what Merkel proposed, or what Thunberg did to save the world.

There was a mood of wait and see. I took mental inventory of the disease scares over the past few decades. There was mad cow disease in the 90s, SARS in the early 2000s, and Ebola and the Avian Flu in 2015. I knew there was a point when these events were all over the news for a few months, and then everyone stopped talking about it. I figured this COVID would follow the same trajectory, and I didn't want to rely on the breaking news media to play with my emotions.

We got the travel green light, and that's all we needed.

Did you know that renting a car for the week in Napoli is cheaper than getting a taxi to and from the airport? It was almost like when I went to the grocery store and saw that the one-liter Coke bottle was only ten cents more than a 330-milliliter can. Was this some sort of a trick? In cases like these, I always grabbed the bigger size.

Within five minutes of driving, I learned that of all the places, Napoli is not the place you want to rent a car. There were too many cars on the dilapidated roads, and drivers made up their own lanes and rules. Traffic lights and lanes were suggestions, and the police officer in the middle of the road was just there for show.

Maricar sat shotgun.

"Can you put your hand out so I can get into the next lane?"

"I feel like I can't move. How close is that car to my right?"

Only 30 minutes into our trip, I was tense, trying not to get a scratch on this new car.

Beyond all the action on the road, the sidewalks swarmed with people crossing when they felt like crossing. With how people drive, I expected pedestrians to be cautious, but they seemed confidently invincible. And then, there were random piles of heaping trash.

"Why is there a mattress and piles of garbage on the sidewalk?"

"I don't know. It wasn't in the brochure. All this is a surprise to me too."

This was a real-life Gotham, and I expected to see Batman chasing down the Joker any minute now.

The traffic congestion faded as we left the city, but the trash remained consistent.

"The mafia?"

"I just looked it up. The mafia has its hand in the sanitation department, and they control it."

"Is this normal for Napoli?"

"It says that it has been going on for decades."

"We aren't in Berlin anymore. Everyone, watch your step."

It was times like these that I appreciated how safe we were in our Zehlendorf, Berlin bubble.

We arrived in our new home for the week. The kids fought for rooms as we put away our things, found Wi-Fi, and turned on YouTube.

"What are we going to watch?"

"We aren't watching a movie so calm down. We are figuring out what we are going to do for the week."

I typed "Rick Steves, Naples," and clicked on the first video. It had over a million views.

Thanks to Rick, we divided our week between Pompeii, the Amalfi Coast, Napoli, and wherever the "eat" portion of *Eat Pray Love* happened. I didn't realize there was much to do in the area, and I forgave myself for renting a car.

Napoli was chilly but warmer than Berlin. Most importantly, it was sunny sometimes. In Berlin, you forget what the sun looks like. Even if we did nothing, getting away from the gray would be worth it.

Driving in Napoli's city center was one adventure, while the Amalfi Coast's scenic drive was on a different level.

An important disclaimer. You should know that I am the worst driver. I'm not in denial. I accept and admit this. It's not because I'm reckless. It's because I lack the skill and confidence. I will park in the farthest possible Costco parking spot, not for fear of others damaging my car but out of fear of navigating narrow parking spots and holding up other drivers.

I don't like roads with no center divider line and cars parked along the sides. I am overly cautious, and my perception is so bad that I slow down to a crawl and wait for oncoming cars to pass.

I've never done a three-point turn. It is at least seven for me.

When I have to parallel park, Maricar knows the drill. She automatically gets out of the car. I roll down the windows and turn off the music as she walks me through the steps with a peeved face. The kids settle in, knowing that just because we are at our destination doesn't mean we are actually there yet.

"Slowly reverse."

"Turn your wheel to the right now."

"A little more."

"To the left."

"Stop."

"Nope."

"Go back. Let's try again."

Travel experts recommend that visitors hire a driver for the Amalfi Coast. Professionals would ensure everyone's safety, allow time to take in the views leisurely, and stop at all the right places for pictures.

Our family doesn't always like to take recommendations.

Pay for a driver when we have our own car? As if!

What made the Amalfi Coast a car enthusiast's dream but my personal nightmare?

For 50 kilometers, there were no straightaways. It's a blind left and right, one after the other.

The drop-off. There was a huge concrete barrier between us and the cliffs, but the thought of our proximity to the drop made me nervous.

The picturesque views were great if you were a passenger, but they were a constant distraction to my goal of getting through this in one piece.

"Daddy, wow! Did you see that?"

"Stop talking to me. I'm trying to concentrate."

It was the off-season, which meant open roads, and I only got honked from behind twice. It's the Amalfi freaking Coast, but the morning sunny weather turned gloomy and windy, and all the stores were closed. We made the most of it by imagining the summer scene and sun-kissed waters. I could see why they called it the off-season and why coming here four months from now would be at a premium.

There were only two lanes. This setup was usually fine until one of three things happened:

1. The oncoming car veered into my lane.
2. Construction forced one lane to close.
3. Someone slowed down, trying to park in a parking spot that didn't exist.

"Can we stop?"

"No. Not right now. We'll stop when we see a parking spot. Enjoy the views."

Somewhere midway through the coast after making our hundredth turn, Feris barely peeped, "I'm not feeling well."

It was a combination of my driving, the roads, and being cooped up in the back of the car. We've been here before.

"Grab the empty chip bag and hold it."

"Got it? Good."

"Hold it there just in case."

Blech followed by another blech. The smell of parmesan cheese began to fill the car. It was now freezing cold and snowing outside, but I opened all the windows.

With my eyes forward and on the road, I called back, "Did you get it in the bag?"

Jero and Lea exclaimed in unison, "she missed!"

They scooted as far to the other side of the seat as possible. Maricar began digging around the car, looking for loose napkins and wet wipes to clean up some slop.

We still had 45 minutes until we got home, and Feris sat there like a statue, coated with the puke Maricar couldn't wipe off. She looked uncomfortable. We rode with open windows for the rest of the ride and became exclusively mouth breathers.

I stuck my head out the window every few minutes to get a clean gulp of air and drove home like I was in a game of *Gran Tourismo*. We reassured Feris we were almost home at least a dozen times for fear she would cry from being grossed out.

The snowfall distracted the other two momentarily, and they began to giggle. I guess they realized they couldn't do anything about it and found ways to pass the time.

The smell didn't go away.

The next day, after my run, I stopped by the market to get the strongest and most toxic chemicals I could find, determined to eliminate the smell. A pet symbol on the bottle was usually a good sign for this job. I oversaturated the fabric and then scrubbed it away. I then left the windows open to let the car air out.

We headed out for the day and walked up to the car. Before getting there, I smelled the fresh spearmint detergent from 20 feet away. I thought, *at least it doesn't smell like vomit anymore.*

When we got in, we got the full blast. The car smelled like a hospital where they went heavy on disinfectant, but the cheesy vomit smell they were trying to cover still lingered.

We still had three days with the car. Fingers crossed that the smell would fade, and we would get our deposit back, but until then, windows down, heater on, and mouth breathing.

Jero and Lea didn't say anything and gave Feris a look of blame.

Maricar told them to cut it out and pulled from her Rolodex of memories, reminding everyone about Jero peeing in the car or Lea spilling milk all over the back seat. Her message? It could have happened to any of us.

For a family where rice is a daily staple, saying we carbed out means *a lot*. Our Napoli daily itinerary involved visiting a historic or must-see site and filling in all the gaps with places Maricar would pull from Instagram or a Google Search. Often, it was one pizza place after another, and they were all good.

The perfection of the pizza was its simplicity and the quality of the ingredients. There was either the Margherita or Marinara, cheese or no cheese and every pie that came out of the igloo-shaped wood-fire ovens carried the distinctive charred spots on the crust.

I loved getting a good deal. The prices we were paying, for the quality we were getting, made it feel like we were eating for free.

"Should we order another?"

"No, we must save room for the next one."

Wisely said by Maricar. She is the voice of reason. If I'm ever in doubt, she steers me in the right direction. Every slice of pizza had diminishing returns. The previous slice always tasted better than the next.

Less than an hour later, we were at the next world-famous-must-go pizza joint with celebrity pictures and awards plastered on the walls. We took a picture of the front and inside with our pizza. We were in carb heaven.

In these places, they don't give you time to relax. You scrambled to find a seat, ordered from the single-page menu, and then your order came out five minutes later. Usually, there was a line out the door and at least a 30-minute wait. The wait would have been nice, giving us time to digest our previous meal and regain our appetite. But no, this was an amusement park without lines. It was like getting to the end of a roller coaster ride, and before getting a chance to unbuckle and unload, the operator asks if you'd like to go again.

How many times can you ride a roller coaster in a row before vertigo sets in?

"I'm thirsty. Can we get a drink?"

"No. You need to save room in your stomach for the pizza. It's the best pizza in the world."

I held the kids off with too many nos. When we ordered water, they couldn't get enough.

"This is the best water I've ever had. It's better than the pizza."

That would be a funny thought if, ten years from now, they forgot about the pizza and only remembered the water. I get it. Sometimes, there's nothing better than a simple cold glass of water.

Finding a bathroom was tough. In the States, you were never too far from a Starbucks. In Germany, clean facilities were everywhere, and it cost less than a euro. In Italy, we weren't so sure.

Before leaving the last restaurant, I issued the usual public service announcement.

"Did you use the bathroom?"

"Yeah!"

"Use it again."

When we explored new territory, every sip came with a warning. "If you drink this, you better be on the lookout for a bathroom and be ready to hold it."

Not even ten minutes later . . .

"I need to use the bathroom."

"I told you to use it before we left the restaurant."

"Hold it. We are almost home."

How does this happen again and again? It's as if the world is using this opportunity to teach children that their parents can predict the future.

We were in the home stretch and crammed in the elevator, going up only two floors.

"I can't hold it."

And at ten years old, Jero peed on himself as we all stood there with him.

I laughed and thought *at least it wasn't in the car, and I didn't have to spend all night cleaning this up, too*. Imagine what the car rental place would think and the stares we would get.

"Go straight into the shower with your shoes and all."

From the elevator, he waddled like a duck.

Fortunately, I still had some of the chemicals from cleaning the car. I showed Jero how to dry his shoes with the hair dryer, and everything was as good as new the next morning.

It was the second to last day of our Italian getaway, and today's adventure included a hike up Mount Vesuvius and a stroll through Pompeii. Per Rick Steves' recommendation, we took the train.

Like in Germany, it was rare to see people of Asian ancestry in Italy. We stuck out. If Germans are known for their adherence to rules, Italians are known for expressing themselves freely and loudly, regardless of what comes to mind. There is no filter.

We find other tourists. They must have watched Rick Steves, too, because we are all heading to Pompeii. We shared the train platform with a large Asian tour group, and on the opposite platform, we heard local teenagers snicker and call out, "COVID!"

"What are they talking about?"

"They are being racist, associating people with a virus."

"What's COVID?"

"It's a virus that has been on the news, but you don't have to worry about it."

Maricar filled in the gaps as we waited for the train. She brought the kids up to speed on what we knew about COVID-19, including where it started, how it spread, and what can happen when someone catches it.

I hadn't been watching the news, but I wondered if this disease was going to stick around and what it would mean for us moving forward.

What did it mean for people of Asian descent? Because Trump was on a mission to poke as many bears as possible, we already tried to downplay our American identity. But our Asian heritage was impossible to hide.

I pushed aside COVID worries and reveled in Pompeii's ancient ruins. From Mount Vesuvius, I marveled at Napoli's bird's-eye view.

History books and movies had primed me for these moments but experiencing them with my family was surreal. We made this happen, and that realization was incredible.

In Their Words:
Napoli, Italy

Jero (10):

- *I heard it was Italy, so I thought it would have the Colosseum. When we got there, it was what I imagined the grimy parts of NYC to look like, with mattresses on the sidewalk and stray dogs.*
- *The food was really good, especially the pizza with buffalo cheese.*
- *Walked all over the place. Eventually, we got to a restaurant and bought expensive water that turned out to be the best water I've ever tasted. I drank so much water that I peed in my pants while in the elevator.*
- *I stepped in poo. I discovered this because I could smell myself while we were on the train. Dad made me wipe my shoes on the grass to get most of it off, and then when we got back to the apartment, I had to clean them.*
- *We hiked up Mount Vesuvius and visited Pompeii. I was excited because I was obsessed at the time with* Percy Jackon & Heroes of Olympus. *I brought the Bushnell binoculars from the Disney Cruise. I remember seeing snow up there and steam coming out of the volcano while we were on it. Pompeii was scary and sad because there were pictures and reenactments of*

dead people. It was quiet, and we mostly had the place to ourselves.

Lea (8):

- *There was a lot of pizza, and we would stay up late past our usual bedtime eating. The crust was slightly burned, too hot, and there was way too much sauce and not enough cheese. Everywhere else we had pizza, there was more cheese.*
- *There were orange trees everywhere along the street.*
- *When we were driving up a mountain, I wanted to open the windows when it was snowing, but Dad wouldn't let us because it was getting the inside of the car wet.*
- *It was a windy day, and Feris threw up on the Amalfi coast drive. Afterward, it smelled like pizza in the car, so I didn't like eating it for a long time.*

Feris (5):

- *It was snowing.*

12
THE ONE-ROOM SCHOOL HOUSE

Berlin, April 2020 (Week 36)

We returned from Italy, and things escalated quickly. The only thing that people talked about was COVID. My initial thoughts that this would blow over were wrong.

Things got real when the stock market crashed in late February, and there were rumors of schools moving their courses online.

We got an email from our landlord. In summary, it said they were cutting their sabbatical short and returning early. They were taking this pandemic seriously and not taking any risks.

Beyond pending news of schools closing, this update had the biggest immediate impact. With our landlord returning, we would have to move from having the entire four bedroom apartment to just one room in the basement. That adjustment would be hard.

As things progressively worsened, Maricar and I had a daily "what does this mean for us?" conversation.

"Do we cut our time abroad short and return home after this school year?"

"If we will be home all the time, how will we be able to survive in one room?"

"How will the pandemic impact our day-to-day? Travel? And, for how long?"

"Why are we out here again? Does the world's new circumstances change that?"

We weighed our options, certain that change would be the only constant moving forward.

We accepted the circumstances and decided to stick with it until the end of the two-year commitment. We would play it by ear, hoping everything would resolve itself in a few months. Who knows?

In the meantime, we focused on what we could control. Having low school expectations and recognizing it would take months for schools to organize themselves, we put in motion a plan to supplement learning by focusing on the core subjects: reading, writing, and math.

We didn't want to add to our frustrations and threw our holiday plans out the window.

Every day was a blur, and it was painful to even think about what we were missing. Instead, we started looking around the neighborhood for microadventures. Alastair Humpreys (National Geographic Adventurer of the Year) who pioneered the concept and coined the term, defines it as "an adventure that is short, simple, local, cheap – yet still fun, exciting, challenging, refreshing, and rewarding."

Before our landlord returned, we had time to decide what to do about our living situation.

We saw two options:

1. Find a new place more conducive to a stay-at-home, hunker-down pandemic existence.
2. Temporarily stick it out until things blow over, and then find a new place.

There were benefits to both, so we explored them simultaneously.

When looking for a new apartment, we quickly encountered some frustrating obstacles. Having a limited grasp of German immediately closed a lot of doors. Making inquiries over the phone had us fumbling for words, and nearly every time, potential leads hung up on us.

This was also just the beginning of the pandemic. People were scared and didn't know fact from fiction, so most people defaulted to being safe rather than sorry. If you thought securing toilet paper during this time was challenging, try finding an apartment. Open houses and in-person contact were things of the past.

With these early trials, staying put was starting to look like the better option. To make it work, we made our space multi-functional so it could be our bedroom, kitchen, dining room, and family room. We "gutted" out the room by replacing the queen-size bed with a sleeper couch and got rid of the large space-sucking desk. We then bought a versatile table that several people could use simultaneously.

When we had the entire furnished 1300-square-foot apartment with utilities, we were paying 1800 euros each month. We negotiated an all-inclusive rate of 500 euros per month for just one room. It was temporary and provided us with the flexibility we needed in these uncertain times.

Still, our negotiation would be a band-aid until the worst was over. We were hoping it would be just until summer.

Maricar had it the hardest. As someone dedicated to her craft and with high expectations, she was already taking steps to ensure her students met yearly standards from a remote teaching setup.

This was all a well-timed wake-up call. We still didn't know the extent of the pandemic's impact, but it drove us to think deliberately about our time abroad. Time and opportunities suddenly became scarce, and the freedom to travel wasn't a given. We had to be deliberate and plan for any challenges that would come our way.

My phone buzzed. It was almost 5 a.m.—time to head out for a run. It was pitch-black outside, but I needed this daily release. Otherwise, my pent-up energy would start a grumpy domino effect, where I would begin snapping at the kids, Maricar would pile on, and then they would take it out on one another. We already had a few lows I was trying to forget it.

Last night, Maricar, Lea, and I fought for space on the IKEA sleeper sofa while Jero and Feris had the floor mats. Lea was a snuggler, so I had to peel her off to avoid waking the whole family. Once I was free of her clutches, I stepped over the other two to not trigger any alarms.

It took just one kid to wake everyone, and then the day started earlier than usual, and there went my alone time. Thankfully, this was not one of those days.

I navigated the dark with a bit of light from the streetlamp outside. This was my routine escape and I learned to manage without using my phone as a flashlight.

Spring gradually replaced Berlin's gloomy and cold winter with more sunlight, a new flower of the week, and slightly warmer temperatures. Still, it was cold enough to feel like winter. My beanie, gloves, vest, and neck buff were in heavy rotation. These accessories had become necessary for keeping my body temperature warm while protecting my extremities. With the weather warming up, I hoped to ditch my beanie by next week.

I'm out the door at 5 a.m. on the dot. I stretched while waiting for my Garmin 35 to catch a signal. I'm off. From Mühlenstraße, I veer right on Hochbaumstraße. My German friend, who I found by stalking on Strava, an activity-tracking app with social features, lived at the end of the street in Lichterfelde West, just a mile from Zehlendorf.

We both left our apartments simultaneously and met somewhere midstride. This was efficient for us both. After meeting, we cut through the *Kleingartens*, small gardens, and Heinrich-Laehr Park as we made our way to the canal for a total of 15 kilometers. On the way home, we split up where we had met up earlier and went our separate ways.

I took a deep breath before heading downstairs into our apartment. It wasn't even 6:30 a.m., so I hoped everyone was still asleep. I opened the door and sighed in relief to hear silence. This meant I might have a few moments of peace before the hive woke up. Guided by the light streaming in, I stepped over Jero and Feris on the floor mats and accidentally bumped into the sleeper sofa. Maricar gave me the universal look to *be quiet.* I nodded and mouthed, "I'm sorry."

The bump was enough to wake Lea. I quickly grabbed my stuff and jumped into the shower, knowing the one and only bathroom would be in high demand in two minutes.

Jero knocks.

"Are you done yet?"

"Give me 30 seconds."

"Hurry up!"

Before stepping out, I threw my running clothes in the laundry. We alternate outfits, wearing just two to three sets of the same clothes. This simplified the process and meant that we were washing every day. I can't start it yet because, according to Berlin's quiet hours, I can't run the machine until after 7 a.m.

Jero and I switched places, and I went into the room to see the two-floor mats folded up and stacked and the four blankets and pillows piled. It was my cue to hoist them above the closets and stuff the remaining bedding away.

The sleeper sofa was then converted into a couch, officially signaling that it was time for breakfast.

To convert our room for eating, we dragged out the bright blue particleboard table to the center of the room. It got a lot of use and even had nail polish to patch up chipped paint. We used two IKEA shoe racks as benches. They weren't intended for people to sit on and had already started bending in the middle, so we used duct tape to reinforce them.

With the constant breaking down and transitioning of our gear, it felt like we were backpacking indoors.

Our north wall was a floor-to-ceiling bookshelf with three columns. We partitioned it out into sections. On the far left, we had clothes, shoes, and toiletries. The far right was for books and school supplies. The middle was our food pantry and dishes.

Our pantry consisted of many carbs in the form of cereals, haferflocken, bread, müsli, and bananas. We had another row dedicated to more carbs in the form of rice noodles, pasta, durum wraps, and rice. The mini fridge was maxed out with seasonal fruit, an Aldi ice cream with a shark on the cover that Maricar craved, Greek yogurt, hummus, spinach, hard-boiled eggs, and as many sausages as we could fit. After nine months, I still didn't know what made a *Weißwurst* different from a *Bratwurst*. It was all sausage to me.

The John F. Kennedy Schule went fully remote weeks ago to deal with the pandemic, and class check-ins began in 30 minutes.

"Time check! Everyone has 15 minutes to finish their food and their morning routine."

Feris, the youngest at five, needed more time to wake up fully. She was complaining about the bananas because they weren't perfectly yellow.

"I don't want to eat a banana. I can see brown spots on the outside."

"It's just the outside. How about you open it up, and if you find any spots, I'll eat them for you."

"Deal?"

"Fine."

She opened it up, and guess what? It was perfectly fine, and I ended up just eating the ends. Another crisis averted. I have learned to spend extra time choosing bananas with a tint of green, so they ripen at the right time. I also ate the spotted and bruised ones in advance.

I opened the screenless window and quickly tossed the banana peel into an orange OBI bucket we used as our compost bin. The warmer weather brewed up a concoction that attracted all sorts of creatures. I shut the window to stop all the heat from escaping and prevent any bugs from coming in. Maricar hates bugs, especially ants. She was always watching me with judging eyes when I opened the window.

"Five minutes."

Jero took too much cereal and *haferflocken*, rolled oats.

"Whoa, whoa, whoa. Where are you going? You still have plenty of food in that bowl."

"I think I took too much."

"Finish it up, and next time, take a little. If you want more, add more. Got it?"

"Okay. Can you take a bite?"

Jero proceeded to scoop out an oversized spoonful for me.

We didn't have a kitchen, so dishes were done in the bathroom with our all-purpose sink. Any bit of food scrap needed to be finished or thrown in the compost bin. A clogged sink would have been disastrous. This is why we were nit-picky about finishing all the food on our plates.

We cleared off the table and put all the dishes into a bin for later.

"One minute."

Maricar taught algebra to eighth graders and had the prime station on the table. Everyone else had a piece of wall as their background and was either sitting on the couch or the floor with their device as they showed their face for roll call.

The school hadn't yet figured out how much time students should spend on Zoom or found ways to encourage interaction. This was a good thing for us. Most of the time, Jero, Lea, and Feris would call in and then disappear.

Our one room apartment was about the size of a parking lot space, a 12' x 22' area, so each person was only a few feet away from the next. If everyone were talking at the same time, it would sound like a call center, and nothing would get done. The Wi-Fi coughed as it struggled to support five devices at once.

I took a moment to survey the scene and tried to process how quickly we went from life at an international school to remote learning in a box. My mantra helped me to take it all in: *you couldn't make this stuff up if you tried*. Lea snapped me out of it.

"Daddy, I need help."

Lea was in second grade, had trouble logging into her call, and was already ten minutes late.

"Why didn't you call me over sooner?"

"I was trying to get your attention, but you looked like you were in your own world again."

"Sorry. Let's see what's going on."

She started to panic as we restarted Zoom and logged back in. It didn't work, so we restarted the computer, guaranteeing another delay. By the time she got on, the call was wrapping up.

Oh well. I rationalized that the teachers and students were used to this. More than half the class had technical issues. Besides the predictable technical problems every time, some students didn't even show up. Even if the check-in calls weren't useful, I ensured my kids were there and made it a part of their routine. If not, the hours of the day collapsed in themselves.

Primary teachers assigned busy work on SeeSaw, which took the kids 30 minutes to complete. Even before the pandemic, primary schools in Germany had a great deal of play with no homework. It was, by design, encouraging social interactions and making school fun. With no in-person sessions, there was a lot of time to fill.

One by one, Jero, Lea, and Feris got off their calls. It was silent as Maricar was still teaching.

Now, the real work began.

When schools started to shut their doors back home, and rumors emerged of something similar happening in Berlin, we put measures in place to be academically self-sufficient. We did not uproot our lives for busy work and would not let the kids fall behind.

I kept a mental timeline. In a little over a year, we would be back in San Ramon, where academic standards were high, and the culture was go-go-go. This whole adventure of living abroad to see the world would be a huge blunder if they got behind in their academics, making the transition back evermore challenging, if not impossible.

I started with Jero and pulled out today's Eureka Math assignment: Module Five, Lesson Two, fractions. We had come a long way in a short time, especially with problem-solving skills and word problems.

The go-to method was Read Draw Write (RDW), a three-step process used in solving word problems that required students to 1) read the problem for understanding, 2) draw a picture or model (e.g., a tape diagram), and 3) write an equation and statement of their answer.

Once Jero and I reviewed the content and completed a few practice problems, he was off on his own, working through the classwork on the outside stairwell to minimize distractions. We had to get creative with space, especially with Jero, who was looking for any excuse to get off task. I then repeated the process with Lea and then Feris.

For writing, I assigned a reflection question. These softball questions asked them to describe their favorite place, food, or movie. The focus wasn't on grammar or handwriting but on getting them comfortable expressing their ideas. At the end of the week, they read aloud their essays, and each person would share something they liked. With the world in flux, it was about putting structure in their daily routine.

With such a confined space for five people, we strongly encouraged being outside. Zehlendorf was a safe neighborhood, so we were never worried about sending the kids out on their own.

"Go for a walk" was something the kids were used to hearing. It had become our solution for nearly everything.

Someone had too much energy? "Go for a walk."

Finding ways to pick a fight? "Go for a walk."

Looking bored? "Go for a walk."

Mommy or Daddy is about to snap? "Go for a walk."

Sometimes, it would be a walk around the block, a small errand like picking something up from the store, dropping off glass at the recycling igloo down the street, or an out and back to a landmark like the Sundgauer Straße station. Regardless of the situation, it seemed like there was nothing a walk couldn't fix.

And in the rare instance that a walk didn't work, we would ensure the next one would be longer.

Our short-term goal was to have our kids work independently so I could start preparing lunch.

Before the pandemic, we had a shared kitchen. I would go upstairs a handful of times a day to prepare our meals and bring them down. During the pandemic, our access was cut off to minimize intra-household contact and the spread of the virus. I had to get creative.

Our Instant Pot became our kitchen. This pressure-cooking workhorse got the job done.

With Maricar still conducting class, I commandeered a portion of the blue table for meal prep and cooking. Today, we were having *phở*, a Vietnamese rice noodle soup, everyone's favorite.

I first soaked the dried rice noodles in hot water and then threw in water, chicken wings, and a seasoning cube into the Instant Pot.

The next step of cutting onions required extra care. There was no vent in the apartment, so circulation was poor unless we opened our windows. We usually do, but the pollen count was high right now, aggravating Maricar's allergies. It was a catch-22. I compromised by cracking the window a tiny bit.

I began cutting the onion and failed to move quickly enough. Maricar, who was the closest, started to tear up, and soon enough, Lea did, too. Knowing I've come this far and can't do anything now, I pushed forward, quartering the onion and threw the pieces into the water. Everyone would be fine in a few minutes.

Maricar was still live on her call. She played off the tears by saying she got something caught in her eye. I can't help but laugh. If only the students on the other side of the screen could see the scene unfolding beyond their view. During the pandemic, each family had to adjust to make life work and I imagined our situation was a bit extreme. I wondered if our kids saw it that way.

After I placed all the ingredients in, I shut the lid and set it for ten minutes. The Instant Pot heated up, and the water inside turned to steam, building pressure. Once it reached maximum pressure, the lid locked, and the timer began.

Ten minutes later, the alarm went off with a beeping sound. I now needed to release the pressure by flicking a knob on the top. When I did this, it would make a loud whistling sound like a hole was punctured in a massive tire. The room would further amplify this sound, drowning out all other noises.

I used hand signals and mouthed a few words to get Maricar's attention. She assigned a practice problem for students to work out independently before pressing mute, and then she gave me a green light.

The release came off like a giant trying to shush the room as steam and an earthy licorice smell followed.

The pressure release was a signal to the kids that we were going to eat in five minutes. They wrapped up their work, lined up to wash their hands, and grabbed a bowl and fork from the bookshelf.

Maricar had an additional ten minutes of class, so we started without her. I tossed noodles into each bowl, and before adding the broth, I sprinkled in some lime, cilantro, and spinach. We attempted to eat in silence.

"Slurp! Slurp! Slurp!"

I gave Feris a look and spoke gibberish with my hand signals.

She got my point.

When Maricar jumped off her call and closed her laptop, there was relief because this meant we could talk freely. The room exploded into talk and laughter.

This chaos had been our pandemic-morning routine for the past month since the world shut down. I reminded myself that we chose this and might as well make the most of it. I rationalized the time spent, believing we were creating unique experiences that the kids would be talking about 20 years from now.

An emerging theme was that timing is everything. We wondered if we had made a mistake. What if we had waited a year? Would we have been able to weather the worst of the pandemic from the safety of our home and start fresh in the fall? If we had the chance to do it all over again, would we take it?

I felt a sense of guilt and questioned my role in all of this, wondering if I was doing enough as a stay-at-home dad to support my family through this difficult time. Were we being punished for our decision? What would become of our careers and personal purpose? Could things get any worse?

Our landlord was just upstairs, separated from us only by an open stairwell. We closed the door and savored our Instant Pot phở as we huddled around our blue table with our makeshift seating.

With schoolwork out of the way for the day, we had a free afternoon ahead of us.

In Their Words:
Our Berlin Apartment

Jero (10):

We didn't have an official door and only had two keys. To get into the apartment, we had to run around to the window and wave. Then, someone would come up to open the apartment building door to let us in so we could go down downstairs to our room. It was embarrassing because people would see us every time we did it.

We had white benches that we used for everything. At first, they were small individual tables we'd use for eating and doing our work. Then, when we got the blue table, we started using them as benches, but they didn't last long. They started to break down in the middle, and we used duct tape to hold it together . . . barely.

The windows had a metal curtain, and I remember burning my hand on the rope because I lowered it too fast. We did it every day, especially during the summer when the sun would come up really early, and it wouldn't get dark 'til ten.

Lea (8):

It wasn't really an apartment—more of a master bedroom. There was a balcony, but to access it you had to walk through a window. There were people in the other part of the apartment. They would call from above, "Do you want to come up and play?" It always startled me because it was a mysterious voice that would come randomly.

Mommy hated washing dishes in the tiny bathroom sink. She complained about it all the time. Before we left, she had Daddy film her washing the dishes. Weird, because if you don't like something, why would you film to remember it?

In Germany, there is a place called Karls, a strawberry farm. We had a strawberry-designed toilet seat cover from there when we moved in. One time, we left on holiday, and they cleaned the apartment, replacing the seat with a normal white one. It was weird and also awkward because she saw the poop stains I made.

In Germany, they sort the garbage for compost, recycling, and regular trash. The worst was the compost. We kept it in an orange Obi bucket outside until it was time to get rid of it. There were maggots and all sorts of nasty things in there. It also smelled. One time, Mommy had to chase me with the bucket because I didn't want to throw it away.

Guitar classes kept going, but we had limited space. Everyone had their designated area. I had the couch. I remember having a stack of worksheets that I would wait till the last minute because they were easy. Not too many calls. It was mostly assigned work.

Feris (5):

We had a couch that turned into a bed, and every night, we'd convert it. There were also two mattresses that we'd have to bring down. We were always fighting for the pink and green pillows and blankets because they weren't the itchy ones.

There was no kitchen or stove, so we used an Instant Pot. We also cooked outside on a white table.

We all had different chores: Garbage, taking care of the recycling, trash, and the compost bucket. Organize. Put all the dishes away. Sweep. It was easy because the place was small, so there wasn't much to do. My least favorite was organizing.

We each had a shelf for our personal items. Manang [a respectful Pilipino title for older sister] *Lea and I had a candy stash that continued to grow and grow from candy we bought from Lidl. When we left, Mommy made us throw it out.*

Had to be quiet at night because Mommy was recording videos for her students. Anytime we'd make a noise, she would have to start over. She would then get really mad.

If we got in trouble, we would have to sit on the staircase steps. Every time we misbehaved; we would have to go one step higher. It was weird because we'd get closer to the top and be visible to the other family. One time, I got in trouble and had to eat there. I dropped my bowl of pasta and spilled my milk because I wasn't good at holding bowls. I then had to clean it up.

To get exercise, we would have to walk to the park and play. We made a lot of friends there. On the way, there was a basil plant, and we'd pick leaves for cooking.

13
MICROADVENTURING IN OUR BACKYARD

Berlin, April 2020 (Week 36)

As we cruised down the road on our bikes, something was creeping up behind us.

"Car, back!" I shouted. "Everybody, get in formation!"

Feris was riding right behind me, followed by Lea, Jero, and lastly, Maricar, bringing up the rear to ensure no one got left behind. With a biking adventure every other day, they had all become comfortable, especially Feris, who only got her own set of wheels a month ago. I was a little sad about my now-empty back seat.

After riding together a few times, we learned that order was important as it kept everyone in line and prevented passing. Everyone knew their place.

I may have run on these roads dozens of times, but biking on them was different. Although there was a risk of cars, we stayed on the road instead of the sidewalk because it was much smoother. This section of the sidewalk had cracks and required a proper mountain bike to navigate the uneven terrain.

If we had a bird's eye view, it would have looked like we were playing a custom version of Nintendo's Paperboy, Berlin edition. Instead of out-running dogs and dodging unmanned lawnmowers, we were trying not to break any cycling laws, avoid getting yelled at in German, and not get bell-dinged by other cyclists.

"How much farther?" Jero hollered from the back.

"We are almost there!"

I didn't actually know. It was hard for me to estimate time with kids. Everything took longer.

"You said that ten minutes ago."

I said that 20 minutes ago, but he didn't need to know that.

"Well, we are closer now," I told him. "Almost there!"

To be fair, Google Maps said it was only a 20-minute bike ride, but with kids, it required taking the longer, safer route, and it took twice, maybe three times as long if we took breaks. We made it to our destination with the usual amount of complaining, no tears, and a few bugs in the face and mouth.

Feris looked exhausted with her disheveled hair and red face. She let out the biggest sigh of relief. It was her longest ride to date.

Jero chimed in again. "Why did we bike all this way?"

I gave him the short answer, "The cherry blossoms. Check them out! You can see them from here."

Everything we saw had a potential history lesson, and I dished it out in digestible bits. Otherwise, their eyes would glaze over. The

Berlin Wall Trail marks the border strip where the wall once stood, separating the former German Democratic Republic from the western part of Berlin. Thousands of cherry trees now lined the border. This trail is called die TV-Asahi Kirschblütenallee am Berliner Mauerweg.

We piled our bikes on the fence and locked them together. As a reward, we stopped at the Edeka and went straight to the freezer section.

At this age, we used a lot of carrots to motivate them on these microadventures. It was now at the point where it was expected.

"Whose turn is it to choose the ice cream?"

Lea spoke up and said, "Me!" She then grabbed a box of vanilla ice cream bars with a chocolate shell. Feris was allergic to nuts, so she knew to pick something she could get everyone to agree on. She wisely chose a pack that looked good and provided the biggest bang for the euro. It came with six. I could see her doing the math in her head.

Daddy will only take a bite. Feris can barely finish one. Mommy never goes for a second. This means that if I can finish my ice cream fast enough, Jero and I will definitely get seconds before they all melt.

"Daddy, this one looks good, right?"

"Sure."

She mischievously smiled and gave Jero a look, knowing they hit the ice cream jackpot. Seeing them working together rather than being at one another's throats was a nice change.

With ice cream in hand and the golden hour upon us, we walked through the rows of trees. They were at a stage where they were about to bloom with a few early flowers scattered about. It was a Tuesday and still early in the season, so there were only a few locals from the neighborhood. The blossoms would open up as the weekend approached and bring the crowds. At that point, it would turn into Disneyland, and taking a picture would be impossible without a crowd of people in it.

With the epidemic, all open spaces had become a needed sanctuary.

"Lea, stop picking the blossoms."

"I didn't pick it. It was on the ground. Someone else must have knocked it down."

She flashed a smirk before running off, and then Feris followed.

She was trouble.

If you asked me, there wasn't anything particularly special about today. It came about because we couldn't stay indoors all day, and there was a place on the map we hadn't explored. So, we went for a bike ride, found ice cream, and walked amongst the trees.

Anytime we went somewhere, there were a lot of questions with an undertone of whining.

"Where are we going?"

"What's there to do there?"

"How long is this going to take?"

"Do we have to go?"

In the end, we would gloss over the complaints, and it would work out. Of course, to make that happen, there had to be some suffering so they would feel like they had earned something, a surprise, or a way to make the experience new, and we had to find a way to end it on a high.

"Today was a good day."

"Yes, it was, Jero. Yes, it was."

I thought things could have been a lot worse, and so far, given our situation, it wasn't all that bad.

It was starting to get dark.

"Let's take the shortcut home."

"Shortcut? Why didn't we do that on the way here?"

"Where's the fun in that? Think of it as taking the scenic adventurous route."

Jero rolled his eyes.

"Everyone ready and in formation? *Los Geht's*—let's go!"

Tomorrow will be a version of today. What changes is what we're cooking in the Instant Pot or what afternoon adventure we're biking to next.

"What are we doing tomorrow?"

"Well, there's a cemetery I've been eyeing on the map, and we'll see if we can find a way in."

"Are we allowed to do that?"

"That's what we are going to find out. And guess what? Supposedly the Brothers Grimm are buried there, and we can find their tombstones."

"Who are they?"

"Only some of the most famous German writers ever. They wrote *Hansel and Gretel, Snow White, Sleeping Beauty, Rumpelstiltskin*, and countless others."

"They sound like a big deal."

"Pretty much."

I left out the part that the bike ride would be twice as long as today. If they knew that, no amount of ice cream would be enough to persuade them.

I made curry for dinner that night and I'm sure our neighbors appreciated the aroma wafting from our Instant Pot.

14
COULD WE DO THIS FOREVER?

Croatia & France, July 2020 (Week 53)

"Have you checked out the Robert Koch Institute Friday report yet?"

"Yeah."

"What are our options?"

"France and Croatia are open."

"Can we do both?"

"Why not?"

"I'm booking tickets."

Four months of isolation, homeschooling, eating the same stuff, making up Berlin microadventures, and restriction after restriction made us in great need of a proper escape.

It was summer, and the worst of the pandemic was behind us. Germany took a deep breath, and the country was ready to move on. We recognized our privilege to travel within the EU while the rest of the world was locked down. We did not take this for granted.

After a Berlin winter, the world came to life, the weather was nearing perfect, and life was grand.

The last four months were about accepting the situation, creating a new normal, and finding a routine in a virus-fearing world. Now, we shifted our mindset to make up for lost time. After all, we were here to explore Europe, and if we had learned anything, time was finite. We had one year left, and the clock was ticking. *Carpe Diem. You Only Live Once.* Call it what you will. The drive was all the same.

Being aware of the clock gave us a motivation that didn't exist before. We went from settling for experiences as they happened to us to aggressively seeking them out and putting ourselves in a position to create them.

School let out, and we were off to our first destination, Croatia.

"Where is Croatia, and what is there to do?"

"Trust me. My friend recommended it, and I've worked everything out. We will be all over the country checking out historic towns, island hopping, hiking national parks, and visiting King's Landing."

Maricar was the brains behind this operation. I was there to drive, ensure we ate, manage the budget, move luggage, and take it all in.

As a baseline, our daily living accommodation was a parking lot-sized room where the walls felt like they were closing in. Since merely leaving our apartment was a win, you could imagine the joy we experienced when we traveled.

"We get our own beds?"

"Yup. You can choose first. At the next place, Jero gets first choice."

"Daddy, you really like this place because of the kitchen, huh?"

"It's pretty great being able to cook with a real pan. Now we can have scrambled eggs rather than hard boiled. Best yet, we don't have to do dishes in the shower or bathroom sink."

"The TV is so big! Can we watch a movie?"

"Sure!"

It beat the experience of huddling together and watching a movie on a 13-inch laptop screen with inaudible sound.

It was as if we were coming out of the stone age and in awe of everything we now had available. The minimalistic and simple lifestyle we had been living gave us a new appreciation for the luxuries we took for granted not long ago. It happened quickly. I now understood why people intentionally slept in the woods for a week and returned with a fresh gratitude for life.

Another dad, Modern Family's Phil Dunphy, once said, "The most amazing things that can happen to a human being will happen to you, if you just lower your expectations."

In Berlin, my morning microadventures evolved from just running to cycling to Schlachtensee Lake, a swim, and a barefoot run. It was liberating and freezing. Yes, *freezing*. The lakes and air temperature didn't quite warm up until late June. I wanted to keep the swimming going, so instead of lakes, I took advantage of the Adriatic Sea, which bordered much of Croatia.

Our first stop on this trip was Zadar, an old town right on the water. Upon arrival, I surveyed the area and tried to work out the logistics for a swim.

Did people swim in the sea?

Was there anything that could sting or eat me?

How would I get in and out of the water?

How far do I have to walk from our Airbnb?

Being the first was never easy.

Back in Berlin, the first time I swam in Schlachtensee, a friend showed me the ropes. It was still early in the season, and I recalled seeing ice around not even a month ago. We went to the lake together, found a spot, and stripped off our layers. He went in first.

I thought to myself, *I can't believe people do this. Aren't they cold?*

I didn't come out here for nothing. If he was doing it, I could too.

It was a quick five-minute dip, just enough to say we went swimming and right before hypothermia set in. Afterward, we toweled off and biked home. The next time and every time thereafter, was easier because I had already done it and each day got slightly warmer.

I was in new territory, and I was alone.

I snuck out while everyone was still asleep. Embracing the minimalist lifestyle, I walked barefoot and shirtless with my goggles and orange buoy through a still-sleeping Zadar. It was a quaint town known for its Romanesque ruins and famous sea pipe organ. As I walked through, I needed to pinch myself because the scene was dreamlike. I strolled up to the edge of the promenade with nothing but a view of the open sea ahead.

*F*** it.* I jumped in.

It's warm. Unlike Berlin, I didn't freeze, and my hands didn't go numb. This was nice.

The saltwater increased my buoyancy, so I needed less effort to stay afloat. And rather than swim with zero visibility in the green algae fog and murky bottom of a natural lake, I was in a saltwater aquarium with plenty of things to keep me entertained. All the visibility got my heart racing as my imagination took over. I began seeing sharks and monsters that would want to take a bite out of me. I blocked out the thoughts and focused on my breathing. *Deep breath in and exhale out. Deep breath in . . .*

I completed my swim along the promenade wall to the end and then worked my way back. I didn't break any records, but I felt like I did something brave. I climbed out using the stairwell. At this point, a few vendors were opening shop, and couples were starting out on their morning stroll. I walked home barefoot, feeling accomplished and excited to cook breakfast for my family in a kitchen with a stove and a pan.

I loved this part of my morning. The access. The convenience. Knowing that I could take my time to enjoy this simple experience brought me joy. A lot of it. Here I was, getting to live the dream. I wasn't in the Adriatic Sea every day, but I had the mindset to do something interesting each day in my new surroundings. These days, it happened to be Zadar and there was plenty to explore.

I had similar opportunities in Hvar. It was a different place and scene, but I experienced that same joy and freedom. Instead of a swim along the promenade, it was in a small alcove adjacent to the multi-million-dollar mega yachts displayed on the main strip.

Getting in and out of the water was tricky. The shores were lined with purple sea urchins or, as Feris described them, spiky landmines. I had never stepped on one before, and I didn't want to find out what would happen if I did. I also didn't feel comfortable asking someone to pee on me.

We didn't have the budget for a mega yacht or fine dining, but we enjoyed our walks, home-cooked meals, and island hopping. Being in the scene and taking time in these surroundings was the win.

In the past, when we went on holiday, it was at most, a week. That became five days when factoring in getting to and from your destination. Even getting to the first day required a scramble of packing and putting in extra time at work to make up for missed days. So, despite being tired, there was pressure to make those five days the most productive, relaxing, and incredible moments. These days, we didn't have that pressure.

We took our time, planned one or two daily excursions and let the rest of the day play out. That ability to go with the flow was priceless.

Croatians wanted to put COVID in the rearview mirror and prioritized living today over fearing the future. Things were back to normal in Croatia, and they had open arms, but borders between certain countries were still closed. What usually was the peak season came with off-season crowds.

Dubrovnik was arguably the most popular and famous destination in Croatia. Most recently, it exploded in popularity because it was the setting for King's Landing in *Game of Thrones*. Maricar and I are huge *Game of Thrones* fans, and we directed the kids as they reenacted iconic scenes, including Cersei's infamous walk of shame.

"Can we watch *Game of Thrones* so we can see what you are talking about?"

"Someday."

"Why not now?"

"It's for adults only. We'll watch it together when you are older."

These were the types of things we'd do to entertain ourselves. We could get pretty creative. Bear in mind our adventures originated with Maricar and me. If the kids were in charge, they would opt to be in front of a screen all day and wouldn't care where we went. But they weren't in charge, and became so accustomed to the exploring lifestyle, that they went with it.

One day, I booked a group kayak tour around Dubrovnik and a nearby island for some father-and-son bonding. Jero and I showed up expecting a fleet of kayaks, but it was just us, another pair, and the guide. Our guide explained that this time last year, there would be 20 kayaks on a tour, with a new one leaving every hour.

Lucky us. A private tour!

These days, the kayaking company felt fortunate to get a sizable morning and afternoon session. I couldn't fathom the impact of the pandemic on the rest of the industry, especially for one so heavily dependent on international tourists.

Wherever we went, people asked, "Where are you from?"

"Germany."

"Your English is really good."

"Thanks. We are originally from California, but now live in Berlin."

For fear of recent political embarrassment and the baggage that comes with being an American, we claimed Germany. People were curious because they wanted to understand which countries had opened their borders and where they could expect tourists in the near future.

Rules and restrictions were changing quickly, and there was hope that things would return to what they once were. Things may have been back to normal in Croatia, but around the world, things were far from it. Even when we tried to forget about the global health crisis, the ongoing impact was everywhere.

Most people were conservative, playing it safe and staying home. We were on the other end of the spectrum, taking our chances and acting like there wouldn't be another time. We experienced guilt, but considering we uprooted our family, it was outweighed by our need to make these two years count. This is one of those instances that I feel affirmed about our decision to accept the travel risk during uncertain times.

The most memorable moment of the trip was a frustrating one that I still shake my head about.

The final leg of our journey was Split, the second-largest city in the country, positioned right on the coast. For every trip, Maricar and I attempted to sneak out for at least one date night while we left the kids at home with a movie. They loved staying home.

"Here's the deal. We are going to go out to eat which means you all get to watch a movie."

"Yea. What's the catch?"

"No catch. As long as you eat dinner without a problem, then we're good."

"Here are your options: *Spongebob: Sponge on the Run* or *The Willoughbys*."

"Can I choose the movie?"

"It has to be a consensus. If you can't decide, you can go straight to sleep."

"You need to be in bed by 10 p.m. And make sure to lock the door."

They knew the drill. And with the carrot hanging over their heads, they were on their best behavior. Easy.

Maricar and I disappeared for a grown-up dinner. I don't even remember what we ate, but I do remember we had a lot of wine.

We returned at a reasonable 11:40 p.m. and climbed the four flights of stairs to our apartment. The landing was an alcove with two other apartment doors. When we tried to open the door with the key, it wouldn't budge.

"Huh. That's funny. Am I turning it the wrong way? You try."

No problem. We knocked quietly. No answer.

"Should we knock harder? There are other apartments here, and it's quiet, we can't be too loud."

"Call them."

No answer.

"Call again."

"Knock louder."

Nothing.

"You think everything is okay? What if there is carbon monoxide poisoning or something?"

"They are fine."

"What do we do?"

"Try again."

Nothing.

"Night on the town in Split?"

"Let's go."

It was 12:29 a.m., and our biggest worry was their safety. Because we had locked the door earlier, we knew they were safe. Yet, as parents, we still had some worries. Getting inside the apartment was our secondary concern. It was too late to reach out to our host or make a scene at the door. We were in no rush and went with the flow.

Less than one hour later, we hit our limit.

"I'm tired."

"Me too. Let's go home and try again."

Heading out for a night in the town was a great idea, but we were getting too old for this. It was well past our usual 9 p.m. bedtime, and we were fading fast.

We climbed the four flights of stairs again.

Ten video calls and 30 minutes of knocking. Nothing.

"Why won't our key work?"

"It's impossible. They have to hear the calls or at least the knocking, right?"

"Should we ask for help?"

We reassured ourselves that they were safe, and out of respect for our temporary neighbors, we refused to break the door down.

We are just going to have to wait it out.

Looking back, we should have called our host for help regardless of the time. But after a certain time of the night and several glasses of wine, all logic goes out the window.

The Wi-Fi reached through the door, and we had the idea to stream *Games of Thrones* since we were stuck outside. We only got halfway through the first episode before our eyes started to close. I forgot what a slow build it was.

We were exhausted and couldn't sleep on these stairs. This sucked.

Time passed slowly in the middle of the night, and by 3 a.m., you would think we would have become desperate. The opposite happened. We made it this far with our suffering. What's a few more hours? We were dumb. If I could go back and whisper in my ear, I would have told myself to do everything to get into the apartment.

We drifted in and out of sleep while sitting upright. At least we weren't cold or in danger.

Looking at the bright side, there was a benefit of being up this early.

"It's almost that time. Let's go watch the sunrise."

"Great idea. We have nothing better to do and by the time we get back, they will welcome us with open arms."

We walked down to the promenade for the third time this evening, now morning. It was still dark and mostly empty except for a few fishermen and the corner pub's janitorial staff. We were early, and like the rest of the evening, we waited. The morning skies were clear, and the sunrise was beautiful, but we were in no state to enjoy it. We were happy to burn 45 minutes and be one step closer to sleeping in a bed.

"Can we head back? They have to be awake by now."

We climbed the four flights of stairs again. We were now knocking and not caring if we made too much noise because the sun was already up.

We kept knocking, and ten minutes later . . .

The door finally opened at 7:02 a.m., and Jero looked half asleep. He was confused and started asking questions.

"Back from your run already? Why are you wearing pants?"

"Don't talk to us."

We walked inside like zombies.

He stood there wondering what he had done and what had happened since we offered no explanation.

We went straight to bed and passed out for two hours before packing and preparing for our flight.

I woke up, and the first thing I did was inspect the door. A deadbolt. I knew it.

I wanted to wrap up our trip differently. Despite all the great experiences in Croatia, this was the one that was the most vivid and the one I retell the most.

In the end, everyone was fine, and we picked up another you-can't-make-this-stuff-up memory. Maricar and I looked back and couldn't help laughing and reliving feelings of frustration.

We returned to Berlin for a week to enjoy the perfect summer weather before shipping off again to France. It was by no means a restful week. We crammed in as many activities as possible, from swimming at the lake to whole afternoons at a Biergarten and family canoeing in circles at the Biosphärenreservat Spreewald. They say that if a family can survive in a canoe and not kill one another, it's a sign of a healthy relationship. After that experience, I believe it.

Every time we got tired and tempted to take it easy, we tapped into our memories of being trapped in our basement and reminded ourselves that our window was closing. Who knew if we'd have another opportunity?

When I imagined France, the only place I pictured was the Eiffel Tower. I had no idea there was so much more. Using the itineraries of friends and travel blogs, Maricar mapped out a road trip that started in Nice and snaked around to Paris. It included stops at Étretat, Mont Saint-Michel, Amboise, Gorges du Verdon, Grotte du Pech Merle, Lourdes, Pyrénées, and Versailles. Maricar did the planning, and I did the driving.

To level up the whole experience, we had one family join us for the trip and another meet us in Paris. The kids appreciated the extra company.

The first leg of our journey was in the French Riviera. Many city names rang a bell from Bond movies or celebrity pop culture—like the Cannes Festival— so I felt privileged to be here. Having our friends around and an accessible beach was a huge early win for the kids. Everything was better with good company.

After traveling along the coast, we went inland. This part of the trip was the highlight for me because it showcased France's beauty. There was the Verdon Gorge, a river canyon with unreal fluorescent green waters where we both hiked along the surrounding rock walls and took a boat through the canyon while daredevils jumped from ledges.

And, when we made our way through the Pyrenees, it was one wow moment after another. The gem was the hike to the Cirque de Gavarnie, an amphitheater-like valley formed by glacial erosion. Several large waterfalls spilled into the cirque. The largest of these was Gavarnie Falls, the second-highest in Europe. It descended some 422 meters over a series of steps before it reached the floor. Every time we look at trip photos, I pause and appreciate its wonder.

Another highlight of the Pyrenees was running through famous stretches of the Tour de France route. As an amateur endurance athlete, I got goosebumps just being in the area. Before leaving the area, I noticed we were close to Lourdes, a major Catholic pilgrimage site. It wasn't on the itinerary, but I knew it would make my mom happy, so we took a mini detour to the Grotto of Massabielle and said our prayers.

We had two northern coast highlights before the final stretch to Paris: Mont Saint-Michel, a tidal island, and Étretat's striking rock formations carved out of white cliffs. The kids thought that the fairytale castle-like appearance and surrounding backdrop of Mont Saint-Michel rivaled Neuschwanstein in the German Alps. In addition to the beauty of Étretat, it also carried additional meaning because it was featured in *Lupin*, a Netflix series we were watching at the time. Despite the heat wave that was upon us, we finished our trip with major highlights in Versailles and Paris.

Our experiences and the kids' memories are often rooted to a particular accommodation. There were two in France that stand out. Coming from the Pyrenees, we drove to Toulouse for a quick overnight before a full day of driving (eight hours) to Pech Merle and Tours. Knowing that we'd only need a place to crash, I booked a last-minute Airbnb from the limited options available.

From the check-in process, I knew this stay was going to be sketchy. We were welcomed into the apartment and shown our room. It had two small twin beds and I barely fit. From what I gather, there was a family staying in the living room and then renting out the two bedrooms while everyone shared the single bathroom. This was not in the advertisement. With the language barrier, it made the whole situation weird.

The other memorable stay was when we made reservations at a hostel near Mont-Saint Michel. After a full day of being a tourist and on our feet, we arrived ready for a shower and to pass out. When I attempted to check-in, we were denied because the kids were under 18.

"Where does it say anything about an age minimum?"

Already late with dusk approaching, Maricar and I whipped out our phones to scan the nearby options. Given the area and the last-minute query, there was nothing affordable unless we wanted to drive an hour away. I went back in, desperate to find a solution. After my persistent back and forth, I learned that their policy didn't allow kids to share a room with others. I proposed booking an entire room with 15 beds for ourselves. It was the most expensive hostel bill I've ever paid, and it's how we got three beds each. The kids were so tired, they weren't interested in switching beds in the middle of the night to get our money's worth.

A snapshot of our trip to France:

- 103 peaches consumed on the road
- 2,968 kilometers over ten days of driving
- Over 200 euros paid in road and bridge tolls
- 21.20 euros for the most expensive toll fee
- 32 baguettes eaten
- 42 wedges of Laughing Cow cheese
- 12 bottles of red wine
- 3124 pictures captured
- 1 baby front tooth lost

We returned a few days before school, glowing with our shared travel experiences. According to the kids, this was the best summer ever, and in the end, that's the opinion that counts.

Maricar and I talked through the plan tirelessly before moving abroad. Two years would be perfect. We would have this little fling with life and return with plenty of time for the kids to settle and jump back on track.

The summer of 2020 was unforgettable.

We were already in our second and final year. Was the end really that close?

"Does it have to end?" I asked Maricar one night.

"This is still just a two-year commitment, right?"

"I don't know. I'm having too much fun, and I feel like we could do anything. Like, nothing is holding us back."

"What would we be doing if we were back in the USA? What are we missing? Probably getting back from an all-inclusive resort in Mexico."

"Why are we doing this again? Has that changed?"

"What else do we need to do? Would one more year be enough?"

"What do you think the kids would say?"

A transformative summer unexpectedly shifted our perspective, unveiling new possibilities. We wondered how much further we could take this story.

Though we had only planned so far, we knew we weren't ready for this journey to conclude.

In Their Words:
Croatia

Jero (10):

- *In Hvar, there was an egg waffle cone ice cream cart along the walkway to our Airbnb, and it cost seven euros. We would pass by the place every day. On our last day, Lea and I convinced Mommy to buy one. It wasn't good. Tasted goopy and sugary. I lied and said it tasted good because I didn't want my parents to think it was a waste of money.*
- *Went on a kayak trip with my dad, and my arms were so tired. We went pretty far out around an island and saw cool things like a bunch of caves. I remember jumping out of the boat to go for a swim. We took a break on a secluded beach for lunch. It was the best food of my life, even though it had tomatoes. Our guide said, "watch this!" He then threw bread into the water, and all the fish jumped out to eat it. I didn't copy him because I was hungry and didn't want to waste the food.*
- *In Split, my parents had a date night. When they went out to eat, we stayed home and watched a movie. Feris was tired that night, and we all went to sleep early. When I woke up the next day, the phone rang, and someone knocked on the door. I opened the door and saw my parents dressed in the same clothes as yesterday. They looked so mad.*

Lea (8):

- *At Hvar, we went to a lot of beaches, and there were warnings everywhere for sea urchins. No one stepped on one, but we saw a lot, especially when we went island hopping. It was one of my favorite experiences. I remember when Daddy swam in a cave while everyone decided to stay in the boat. We then followed and got him out. Stopped at a place where there were lots of tiny pink jellyfish in crystal clear water, and I swam to the beach to get away from them.*
- *At Dubrovnik, we stayed at a place with a walled village below. Mommy wanted to walk on top of the wall, and it is what I imagined stepping on the Great Wall of China would be like. The Airbnb had a small pond where I fed the fish. I pulled one of the fish out of the water. From that point on, that fish was scared of me and stayed under a rock when I would come close. It was traumatized.*

Feris (5):

- *I remember a speed boat and going island hopping. One nice place was a blue and green cave. I learned that if you ever get a sea urchin that stings or pokes you, you need to have someone pee on it.*
- *We went into a cave where the water was teal and cold. Mommy made me get in because she said we paid for it.*
- *We stayed in a white house with a pink bougainvillea plant*

covering the entire front. There were a lot of steps we had to climb to get there. Kuya Jero [Respectful Pilipino title for older brother] *and manang* [Respectful Pilipino title for older sister] *cooked eggs.*

In Their Words:
France

Jero (10):

- *I was excited because this was a big trip we were doing with other families.*
- *There were 20 Lego pieces I found with my friend, James, in a restaurant, and we took turns. We used them to build different things like ships, which was my entertainment the whole time.*
- *Circle Falls was one of my favorite hikes that we've ever done. It was scenic and open, and there were several different routes—an adventure! In one section, I walked through a river, dropped my shoe, and it got washed down. Luckily, it got caught on a rock, and I got it. It was the summer, but there was a glacier there. There were sheep with body paint marking them. They kept the sheep contained with walls of rock, and each had a bell on them.*
- *I ate escargots in Paris. I forgot what the reward was, but it motivated me to do it. It came with a small special fork with two prongs. Use it to poke the snail and pull it out. I don't even remember the flavor because I followed it up with a bunch of fries.*

Lea (8):

- *My favorite place was Nice. It was nice. Went with the Steeles. There was a gigantic beach that ran along the whole coast, and it had a lot of rocks. Swam super far with a pool noodle along the beach, and there were lots of fish you could see through the clear water. We eventually came back because we got hungry for pizza.*
- *Verdon Gorge. The water was really green. Teal. I couldn't see anything, but it was really bright and pretty. We did a hike and then went to a swimming river area and hung on to a mossy rock. We pretended to be stuck so we didn't have to hike anymore because it was very dry and hot.*
- *The one thing I wanted to do was eat macaroons because I like them. I didn't get to do it.*
- *The Eiffel Tower looks like a triangle. I never noticed that there was a ball at the top. It looks like a transmitter that can send signals to aliens.*
- *I think the square thing with a bell and circle* [the Arc de Triomphe de l'Étoile] *around it was better, especially for taking photos since you can see the Eiffel Tower from it.*
- *Didn't go inside the Louvre even though I would have liked to see the Mona Lisa.*

Feris (5):

- *Went to the Eiffel Tower. I wore a white fluffy dress with three flowers. I was hot, itchy, and sweating.*

- *While we were there, I lost a front tooth. I was then missing both front teeth, so I looked like a bunny.*
- *Visited a castle* [Mont Saint-Michel] *and had to walk around it through all the mud. I started crying because the mud felt gross and was squelching. The tide just left or was coming in. I just wanted to stop. We went inside the castle to visit the Steeles who were staying in the hotel and walked around but we didn't stay there.*
- *We went to a lavender field, and I threw up on the way. There was only one tree in the field and lots of bees flying around. I'm not sure if it was still a lavender field because they all were recently cut. It smelled like one of those strong perfumes.*

15
TRAVELING ON BORROWED TIME

Greece, October 2020 (Week 66)

There was a correlation between colder temperatures and positive COVID cases. At least, that was the talk around the parent round-up this morning.

"The second wave is coming."

"The second *what*?"

"Wave. That's what they are calling it. You didn't think this was over already, did you?"

"I sort of did."

"Rumor has it that governments were expecting this and will be pushing out new restrictions."

I had family in the US, and they started the school year with remote learning as if it were expected. But that was there, and so far, they have done a terrible job handling the pandemic. I wouldn't say Germany figured it out, but we've certainly done better to keep infections low. I was hoping we would keep it that way. After the summer, it would break my heart to go back to mandatory lockdowns and curfews.

Maricar arrived home from school, and I shared the gossip.

"It's the same rumblings I'm hearing from other teachers."

How quickly our blissful summer high reset. Maricar and I looked at one another, recognizing we were thinking the same thing:

Could we squeeze in another trip before we get stuck?

We talked through the details.

"What are our options?"

"Did you see Friday's Robert Koch Institute's travel page?"

"Our options are Vatican City, Switzerland, and Greece. Slim pickings," said Maricar.

"And, regardless of where we go, we'll need to get tested before leaving and fill out a whole bunch of paperwork."

"They aren't making it easy," I said.

"Let's assume the worst is going to happen. There will be another outbreak, we return to remote learning, and all travel is *Verboten*, forbidden. If that's the case, let's go!"

"Where?"

"I don't care. Anywhere is better than being stuck in this box, especially when we could be somewhere else. This is our last year."

It was as if the government put testing, tracking, and additional restrictions in place overnight to contain the virus. We went from everything being fine to a government-sanctioned lockdown.

The government allowed travel between Germany and other countries based on confirmed positive cases per 100,000 which would be updated and officially posted every Friday. The rule of thumb was that if a country had better numbers than Germany, it was open for travel.

Options were limited, and details would change weekly. Because this was new for everyone, including those making and enforcing the rules, we often learned about policy changes that would go into effect immediately. It was stressful, but we were motivated and resourceful.

We often were in doubt.

Should we even be traveling? Are we missing anything? What if we caught the virus while in another country?

Looking back, it is hard to believe what we willingly put ourselves through to travel. Out of context, people would say we were reckless and unsafe, but knowing our motivations, timetable, and the alternative, we would do it all again.

We decided on Greece for the two-week *Herbstferien*, fall break, and started a checklist. The days of merely packing your bags, bringing your passport, and catching a flight were over.

Official testing for travel was new, expensive, offered only in select locations, and inconvenient. The price per person was 50 euros. As a family of five, that meant 500 euros round-trip. We saw it as a heavy tax.

We blocked off three hours to get tested. That gave us enough time to find the place, stand in a queue, and then get tested, which often took less than a minute. An important requirement was that tests had to be within 48 hours of the flight, or they wouldn't let you board. What happens if the test was positive, even for just one person in the party? There goes the trip. No refunds.

In addition to a negative test result before flying, each passenger was required to fill out an online form at least 24 hours before a flight. It asked standard questions like:

"Where are you staying?"

"Have you had COVID?"

"Do you have any of the following symptoms?"

Once a traveler completed a form, they issued a QR code within 24 hours.

Vaccines were still a long way away, and all these measures were a stopgap. The world was trying.

Filling out a form well before arriving in a country was a recent change, and the process was clunky. For the record, I filled out the form. I double-checked and triple-checked, but it didn't allow me to add additional people to my party.

No worries. Like a custom form, you just need only one per party, right? Being American, we were used to everything being in a gray box and assumed we could talk our way through anything, but these were different times.

"Ring!"

School let out, and we went through our departure checklist.

- Passports

- Tickets
- Paperwork
- COVID tests
- Masks
- Clothes and bags
- Toiletries
- Accommodation confirmations
- Transportation to the airport mapped out
- Transportation to the hotel confirmations

I even had a cleaning checklist for our one-room basement apartment before we left. There is nothing worse than coming back exhausted to a place in disarray.

We were getting good at this.

It was raining, so I ordered a taxi, and we got to Berlin's Schönefeld Airport early to take advantage of our new lounge access. This perk of all-you-can-eat-and-drink became the highlight of any trip for the kids.

"Can I get two drinks? One for now and then another for the plane?" Jero asked.

"Good idea. While you are at it, you should grab two croissants," I winked.

On EasyJet, they stripped down the flight experience, so every request was an overpriced upgrade. We took our time and enjoyed the lounge for every moment before we had to queue up.

Greece, here we come!

Our first stop would be the off-season party island of Mykonos, then we would ferry over to the postcard-popular island, Santorini, before finishing with a trip to Athens to check out all the historic sites.

We hopped into the queue with the other passengers and had all our paperwork in hand to streamline the process.

The kids started their usual banter:

"Where are our seats?" Feris asked.

"Can I sit next to the window?" Lea asked.

"Which movie do you want to watch first on the iPad?" Jero responded, ignoring Lea.

It was our turn.

"Are all members of your party present?" the TSA agent asked.

"Passports?

Boarding pass?

COVID tests?

QR code?"

"Where is the QR code for everyone else?" asked the agent.

"Well, you see, when I completed the form online it only allowed me to add my name," I tried.

"The name of every person in your party has to be on this sheet, or we can't let you on the plane."

"Okay, let me write their names down."

"No, sir, it has to be printed on there."

"Can I show you a digital version?"

"Yes. That will work."

"Give me one second."

They were being firm with no wiggle room. What was I thinking? This was Germany, where rules matter, and everything was in black and white. I could feel my heart rate racing as I tried to devise a solution.

After ten minutes of refilling the form online and with every other passenger through the gate, I showed them the submission.

"I got it."

"Sorry, sir. Their names need to be on the official form from Greece. This just shows that you submitted your paperwork for the rest of your party, but it still needs to be approved and a QR code needs to be issued. I can't let you on the plane without the QR code."

She was firm.

I responded desperately. "Give me one second. I will write down everyone's name on the form and show it."

"As I mentioned, it has to be printed. I'm sorry, sir. We are closing the gate."

My Hail Mary at this point was to doctor the document online by adding everyone's name and then show it. I had a phone and an iPad but no experience. It was too late.

They closed the gate, and Maricar's eyes watered. One other person wasn't allowed on the plane. She looked dumbfounded and shocked and then started to cry as her mascara ran down her face.

I couldn't believe they didn't let us on the plane.

Jero was confused and began asking questions.

"Why wouldn't they let us on the plane? Are we going home now?"

He couldn't have chimed in at a worse time.

I snapped and gave him a short response.

"Don't talk to me right now. Go play over there by the snack bar while Mommy and I figure this out."

Maricar and I gave each other the *now what?* look. We couldn't believe that just an hour ago, we were riding the high of going to Greece, and now we were stuck in the terminal. We took inventory of the situation as I sighed and replayed the scene of what just transpired.

I mumbled aloud.

"I screwed up and didn't fill out the form properly."

"Where was the option to add more people?"

"Hotel reservations were nonrefundable."

"Flights were nonrefundable."

What else?

Greece was one of the only countries open for travel, and we wanted to leave Berlin for the break.

"Is this a sign that we should stay?"

"If not Greece, where?" asked Maricar.

With our emotions still high, we put everything on the table to identify potential solutions given our priorities.

We concluded that Greece was our only option, and if we focused our efforts, we could find a way there. The area was now deserted, so we thought in peace.

I took a quick glance, and the kids had found a way to entertain themselves. We looked up plane tickets from Berlin to any destination in Greece. The few options available were expensive and inconvenient.

"Oh my god! 1500 euros per person?" I said in surprise.

"On EasyJet, we had tickets for everyone at that price."

Every search was disheartening. And with a family of five, the cost ballooned quickly.

We spent 30 minutes browsing our phones before finding tickets that could work.

"I think I found something. Have you heard of GoToGate?" offered Maricar.

"Give me one sec. Let me check."

I searched Google and a list of recommended search queries came up. The first recommended search was "Is GoToGate legit?" I skimmed the write-up.

"It seems okay. How much is it?"

"The price isn't bad. It's the runaround I'm worried about."

"The runaround?"

"It has us flying out tomorrow night to Dublin, Ireland, which is nearly 1000 miles in the wrong direction. We would arrive late in the evening, and then we'd have a six-hour stop over to catch a 5 a.m. flight. We would lose at least a day, likely not sleep, and be out the cost of new tickets."

"Unless we wanted to pay three times this amount, I don't see a better option."

"You lost me at '1000 miles in the wrong direction,' but I haven't been able to find anything else that works. Let's do it!" I said.

We purchased the tickets, and it was unclear if it went through.

Was everything against us today?

"Did you get an email confirmation?"

"Not yet. "

"I searched again, and the tickets are now 50 percent more!" *What happened?*

I tried calling GoToGate, but there was no number, so I emailed them. No wonder people were searching if GoToGate was legit!

After what felt like an eternity but was only ten minutes, we received an email saying our request was being processed and may take 72 hours.

"That's helpful. What are we supposed to do with that information? Our flight is soon."

While we waited for some sort of receipt or ticket confirmation, we resubmitted our forms for Greece and triple-checked them together. I saw the "hidden" option to add more people.

After another ten minutes, we received our ticket confirmations from GoToGate. I was starting to feel better with the momentum and a path forward.

I called the kids over from their makeshift play area.

I explained what happened.

"I'm sorry about how I acted. I messed up filling in the form, and they wouldn't let us on the plane. I was stressed out."

I then explained our workaround solution.

"It's okay. Can we go home now?" asked Lea.

It was amazing how quickly the kids could brush things off and move on to the next thing. I on the other hand replayed the mistakes I made that put us in this situation and then visualized the logistics so we wouldn't have any more missteps.

It wasn't even 10 a.m. yet, so we took the bus. As minimalists, we traveled light and only had carry-on bags. We were grateful for this habit because if our stuff had been flown to Greece, we would have had another problem to deal with.

On the ride, I thought about the potential roadblocks:

Wasn't Dublin on the restricted list? Could we fly to Dublin from Germany?

If we flew from Dublin, would we be allowed into Greece?

Dublin wasn't an approved city. Was a five-hour layover considered a visit to Dublin?

If we flew to Dublin, would we be allowed back into Germany?

We had to ask because the cuts were fresh, and we knew parts of the UK and Ireland were on restricted travel lists. I did not want any more drama.

The next day, we went to the other Berlin airport, Tegel, and got in line to board the plane to Dublin. We had all our paperwork ready and were first up. If something went wrong, we would catch it early and adjust before they closed the gate. As they reviewed our paperwork, my heart felt like it was about to pop out of my chest.

"Please head on through."

I sighed in relief.

The flight to Dublin was easy, and we arrived at 11:15 p.m., a solid six hours before our next flight. Lounges were closed, and we were afraid to step outside the airport. The only seats available were the stiff metal chairs in a well-lit area. They really didn't want passengers getting comfortable and sitting too long.

Other than us, there were a few individuals scattered around the airport who I assumed would also be our bunkmates tonight.

After seeing our options, I realized this was going to suck more than I thought. I imagined sections with sofa seating and dim lighting. This was far from it.

At least it was clean and looked safe.

I made a few laps around the airport, determined to find a spot that was better than the metal chairs and wasn't lit up like a baseball field.

I played out other options in my head:

Could we lie on the floor? That would be a no from Maricar.

Could we get a hotel? By the time we got there, it would be time to turn back. We were already over budget, and what if we couldn't travel back to Germany?

I made three loops again and came back with no good options.

Boldly, I wandered into a closed-off section of the airport. I moved a stanchion and found a deserted food court. It was either closed because it was late or because of pandemic protocols. Regardless, I thought I had hit the jackpot and excitedly brought everyone to our new hideout.

I found some moveable cushioned booths that allowed us to lie down. Compared to the other fluorescently lit areas, it was relatively dark. I smiled and showed them my find.

"Daddy, is this allowed?"

"Absolutely. If you don't like it, you can try and get comfortable on the chairs over there."

I pointed to the other option.

In this situation, I would ask for forgiveness rather than permission.

Maricar hesitated, but the lack of sleep and the limited options made it a great idea. We threw our jackets on top of ourselves and settled into a Tetris-like sleeping formation. The kids found a way to pass out.

I got an hour of sleep, maybe. Every sound made me open my eyes. I was afraid someone would come by to tap me on the shoulder and tell me we had to go.

No one ever came.

We made it through the night and woke up with the airport humming back to life. Lights turned on, and the cleaning staff were getting to work.

"That wasn't too bad, right?"

We picked up our boarding passes and went straight to the gate.

Here we go again. We approached the gate, and my heart rate began to build as I imagined the worst-case scenario. What if we got stuck in Dublin?

There were two lines at the gate. The person on the left moved more efficiently, spending just a few seconds with each guest before letting them through. We went there.

When it was our turn, I walked up as stiff as a robot and held my breath. I was certain I looked suspicious.

I made eye contact and tried my best to play it casually.

"Please enjoy your flight."

Those words were music.

We were finally on our way to Greece.

I turned to Maricar and flashed her a smile.

"That was easy."

Our first stop when we arrived in Greece was immigration. They didn't check our paperwork and I wasn't sure if I was relieved or disappointed. If I had only filled out the form correctly or the first attendant had let us through, we could have avoided all this drama.

I almost forced immigration to check our paperwork to validate the detour we had just endured. I bit my tongue and moved on, unwilling to poke the bear and take a chance.

Greece was worth it.

It was the off-season for two reasons: 1) It was the start of fall, and 2) it was the height of the epidemic for the rest of the world, but Greece was considered "safe."

Being here during the off-season meant that places usually crowded with tourists were abandoned.

Mykonos' usual party island vibe was a shadow of its usual club atmosphere, at least from what I had seen on social media. Our days were laid back and quiet, with extended breakfasts, long walks along a different beach each day, and frequenting the only one or two open shops in the area. It was nice having little to do while having a lot of time to do it. Besides the strong winds that shortened a beach day and made for the rockiest five-hour ferry ride of our lives, the weather was pleasant for this time of year. I heard we lucked out.

Our holiday pace picked up when we took a ferry to the more popular Santorini Island and the city of Athens. Visiting each place was one highlight reel after another. Having Thera's wall of white houses with blue domes and the Parthenon in the background of our pictures made everything look photoshopped.

Because we were bold enough to make the trip, we shared these experiences with locals rather than with the massive cruise ships of tourists that, before the pandemic, would swarm these bucket list destinations. Every day felt like an easy Sunday with the family.

We believed the world would shut down again and this was our last chance to get away. Our invested emotional capital made the swings heavy. There were the trip anticipation and Greek adventure highs to the airport fiasco lows. Being denied at the gate was an inconvenience and a blow that hurt.

One of my favorite quotes, from the unlikely source of Mike Tyson, is: 'Everyone has a plan until they get punched in the face.' We were hit hard, left stunned and disbelieving for 30 long minutes. We were rejected at the gate, viewing the situation through Eeyore's gloomy lens. But we snapped out of it, explored our options, and found a way to make it work. This experience reminded me of how well Maricar and I work together, sharing priorities and resourcefulness to achieve our goals.

I was impressed by how well the kids adapted to the situation, either trusting us to figure it out or unfazed by the uncertainty of our travel plans.

As travel became increasingly complicated, I wondered if it was still worth it. But the uncertainty and challenge of making it happen only made the experience more deeply appreciated.

In Their Words:
Greece

Jero (11):

- *We would hang out on the beach all day. For dinner, we would stop at a sandwich place to get mini baguettes and yogurt.*
- *There was a walk we would have to take from our apartment to get to the beaches and the more touristy areas. Most of the places were closed already. The walk felt like it was just yesterday. I remember it so vividly.*
- *In Santorini, I think I celebrated my birthday here. I was afraid because my parents said we were doing a big hike. They are always making us do stuff like that.*
- *Went to a restaurant for dinner, and afterward, my mom dared me to swim to a buoy when it was pitch black and wavey. I remember she said that if I did it, then I'd get unlimited screen time. It looked dangerous, so my mom changed her mind and said, "if you go in, you get an hour." I went back the next day after a run and did the swim.*

Lea (9):

- *A local mama from Mykonos ran our hotel and would bake moist cakes that we would eat for breakfast every morning. They were the best. Sometimes, she would sneak me an extra one. After a few days, we started referring to her as Mama's best friend because she reminded us of our Mama Espie back home.*

- *Everything from our hotel was a hike, even to the beach.*
- *We were supposed to do a two-mile hike, but the gate to the start was closed. I was happy because I thought it would then be shorter than expected. Mommy found another way, which turned our original two-mile hike into five miles. I wasn't happy about that.*
- *Visited a lot of different beaches with clear water. I remember Daddy made me rank each one. At one beach, we built a fort using all the materials around rocks, sticks, and sand. It was an Oobleck fort that lasted two days. I wish we could have spent more time working on it.*
- *Went to Athens from Santorini, and I remember how bad the ferry ride was. It was rocking so much that I threw up all over the table. It was pink and smelled sour. Athens was a huge tourist attraction, and there were a lot of souvenir shops. I still have the magnet of a famous monument with columns we got from our Airbnb host. It's like the Brandenburger Tor columns.*
- *I don't remember the food except for the tiramisu that Mommy liked. That's where I learned about that yummy dessert.*

Feris (6):

- *We slept on red couches at the airport. We were cramped. I was cold and didn't have a blanket. I was really tired. I don't know why we were there.*
- *Stayed at a place with a lot of blue. I brought the cards, and I remember playing solitaire on the bed. I was still learning, so I cheated a lot.*
- *There were a lot of mosquitos in our hotel. The food at the hotel was so good, and it was all cooked by one Grandma. They had a pool with a lot of floaties like sharks. I didn't know how to swim yet, so I used my arm floaties.*
- *We visited a stadium* [the Panathenaic Stadium] *and stood on the podium. There were also a lot of stairs, so we ran up and down them.*

16

COVID IS BACK, AND IT'S DARKER

Berlin, November 2020 (Week 70)

We've seen this before.

Not only was winter coming, but COVID was back. This meant a double whammy of progressively shorter, darker, and colder days, along with all the restrictions and isolation that came with a global health crisis.

The first time the virus hit, it all happened so fast. It was an initial shock, followed by reactions to a quickly changing world.

This time, it felt like rewatching a lousy movie we had seen before and were forced to watch it on loop. The pandemic dragged on, and one rotten experience followed another.

Zehlendorf is the home of the John F. Kennedy Schule (JFKS), a through school offering integrated, bilingual education for German and American children. It was part of the former post-WWII US sector and had many American influences. One of those was celebrating everyone's favorite American holiday: Halloween. It seemed not to exist anywhere else but the four blocks along Luchsweg. Families from all over Berlin descended onto these streets to revel in the over-the-top decorations and free candy. Last year, it was a welcome taste of home.

"Can we go trick or treating again at the same place? We should get there early this year because a lot of the houses ran out of candy."

"Sorry. I got some bad news. It's canceled."

"Really?"

"There was a parent thread on the topic. It looks like they are shutting down any in-person event, even if it's outdoors."

"What are we going to do?"

"We'll eat ice cream, carve pumpkins, watch a movie, and call it a night."

This was just the beginning of a string of disappointments and not-so-happy memories.

One of the highlights of the JFKS music department was their violin program. They would take students at the entrance class level—the American equivalent of kindergarten—and build them up over time. It was quite exclusive and required an early commitment. We felt lucky when Feris was able to get in.

For the first three months, they would play on a homemade art project consisting of cardboard, wrapping paper, and a ruler, which served as a violin stand-in. Feris graduated to the real thing, but unfortunately, two weeks after she got her real violin, in-person classes stopped, and she never learned how to play. That was over six months ago.

She had the violin, maybe one or two lessons, and it was now collecting dust as we paid the monthly rental fee.

"Feris, why don't you try playing? Maybe classes will start again and having some practice is better than none."

I think Feris only agreed because she had nothing better to do.

Having no experience, I tried to direct her to hold it and position her arms. I played the music as she moved the bow and attempted to keep the rhythm.

In our one-room apartment, where everything echoed, she screeched along. Jero and Lea suddenly were motivated to go outside.

"Do I have to keep playing?" she asked.

"Five more minutes. Don't worry about the sound of the violin, just get comfortable holding it and moving to the rhythm of the background music."

There's a saying that most kids don't stick with the violin because their parents are the ones that give up first. I wanted her to stop, but I wanted to be supportive, and I knew we had to start a routine.

She didn't make it five minutes.

A random neighbor strolled up to our window and started shouting angrily in German. I couldn't determine what he said, but I got the message.

I turned red and was embarrassed. I forgot it was Sunday, which meant *Ruhezeit*, quiet hours. I forgot that it also applies to music.

That was the last day Feris ever picked up the violin.

At this point, kids were in school for half-days. Maricar, as a teacher and perfectionist, was trying to find the best set-up for her lessons.

After trial and error during the first wave, she learned that recorded lessons and tutorials paired with live optional office hours worked best. It provided students with flexibility and addressed many technology and attendance issues that often sprung up.

To pull this off, Maricar would spend at least an hour each day recording videos that she would later send out to her students. We had to be absolutely silent because any sound would get picked up, and she would have to re-record.

Have you ever noticed that when you are in a group, and someone tells you to stay quiet, every action seems to be the funniest thing ever? This is what it was like while I tried to keep everyone quiet while Maricar recorded her videos. It took a few times before I learned it was useless, and we had to leave the apartment.

Another challenge with the set-up was that Maricar would ferry between school and home with photocopied papers and work. And because every mile mattered to reach her mileage goal of 2020 and to keep her annual streak alive, she would often run with papers as she made her way between the school and apartment.

On one of her many commutes home, as the sun set closer to 4 p.m., and with her hands full, she tripped face-first onto the cobblestone streets. Her front tooth hit the ground in the worst way, and she instantly looked like Lloyd Christmas. It was bad.

"What am I supposed to do?"

"I think you are supposed to put it in milk."

"Put what in milk? I don't know where the rest of my tooth went," Maricar said.

"The office is closed, but I can call them tomorrow for you," I responded.

"I'll just go there."

"You should at least take a picture. You know, for the scrapbook."

"Stop it."

Because of the language barrier, getting any professional service was a headache. It would come with inquisitive and impatient questions to which we did not know the answers. We would often walk out unsuccessfully or with an appointment for one month later. That's why we tried so hard to stay healthy and avoid going to the doctor or dentist unless it was an emergency.

Maricar was committed. I would be too if my smile looked like that. She woke up early the following morning and put on her running clothes.

"Are you going to the dentist like that?"

"That's the plan. I figure if I show up like this and point to my chipped tooth, they will feel sorry for me and see me right away."

"If I understand correctly, you are going to play a game of charades. They have to guess that you went for a run, fell, chipped your tooth, and now need an emergency dental repair. It makes sense to me."

This is the stuff we would do because we couldn't speak the language. I felt the pain of all the people in the US who spoke English as their second language.

Maricar returned later that morning and flashed her new smile to the kids.

"I can't even tell which tooth it was."

"I told you it was going to work."

Last Thanksgiving, we went to Austria's Granstein, relaxed at Aqua Dome, and experienced our first *Weihnachtsmarkt* at Innsbruck. We had *Glühwein*, mulled wine. What would we do this year?

"We've got to plan something," Maricar said.

"It's cold. All hotels are closed. Restaurants don't allow in-person dining. Travel between states is restricted. Did I mention that it's cold?" I responded.

"Hamburg is open, and I've always wanted to visit."

"It's something different. Let's do it."

We filled in the kids and got them on board.

"Where is Hamburg?"

"It's northeast of here and about two hours away."

"What are we going to do there?"

"Explore and eat HAMBURGers."

"Explore? Doesn't that mean walking?"

"Pretty much. It's better than staying here. I promise, it will at least be memorable."

Cabin fever was setting in, and I was happy to go anywhere other than Berlin. The catch was the cold. By this time of the year, it was freezing—the type of cold that would cut through your layers. This meant that even if properly dressed, you could only be outside for so long.

We caught the early train to make the most of our day trip. It might have been too early because the downtown area was still asleep when we arrived.

Berlin in November was cold, but Hamburg seemed much colder with its wind chill. We were in for a long day.

There was no seating, even at restaurants, and it seemed like they blocked off anywhere to sit in the city. I assumed this was the city's compromise to open their doors while preventing people from loitering.

True to my word, we did a lot of exploring, walking, and eating while standing. Maricar led the way as we braved the cold and logged a half-marathon of distance.

There were two highlights:

First, Hamburg was known for its bridges and tunnels. We walked what seemed like forever to see a famous bridge in Speicherstadt. There was a cheer from the kids when Maricar announced we made it.

Then, the kids chimed in:

"That's it? I don't get it."

"It's famous."

"For what?"

"Just enjoy it."

"Enjoy what?"

"Can we take a picture and go get ice cream now?"

The second highlight was the train ride home.

If the option was available, we would have caught an earlier train. Exhaustion had taken its toll on all of us. But finally, sitting on a warm train for two hours felt like a luxurious reprieve - the highlight of our day.

It was November, and let's just say it had been a grueling couple of weeks for everyone. Our spirits were at an all-time low, and we desperately needed a boost. With Christmas markets likely closed for the season, we wondered if there was anything left to look forward to.

In Their Words:
COVID Life

Jero (11):

- *I didn't really mind. Using Zoom was annoying. When I unmuted myself, I would have to get the attention of everyone else in the room to let them know I was about to talk.*
- *We got less work when we were out in Berlin. Most of the stuff was pretty easy, and I would have more time to play with Felix, Campbell, and Jakob.*
- *We'd play ping-pong after lunch at the different nearby parks.*
- *PE class online was useless because we were indoors, and it wasn't fun. We'd get homework, and I remember getting good at jumping rope. I was the best.*

Lea (9):

- *Our neighbor put up a plastic sheet between our area and theirs so that germs wouldn't spread.*
- *School days were cut in half, and there were fewer students in the classroom. They stopped serving lunch because of the shorter days, so that they would pass out white paper bags of food. Sometimes, there would be good pastries, like a spinach croissant.*

- *Before things got really bad, they would call pairs into the gym for testing. They would pull you out of class, and it wasn't that bad.*
- *We were there for a bit before COVID, so it was difficult to compare. In the second year, we were much more comfortable with the area and knew what to do.*

Feris (6):

- *I would have to wear the adult masks, and it looked weird because they were so big on my face. I had to wrap it around my ears twice so it would stay on.*
- *During snack time, we would watch comic dinosaurs to keep us entertained. My teacher's name was Mrs. Dogma, but we called her Doggie. That was first grade. Mrs. Viola was my kindergarten teacher.*

17

THIS CAN'T BE THE END

Berlin, November 2020 (Week 72)

"We can't go back." I said. "It feels like we just got started."

"It's not over yet. We've got nine months. Babies are created in that time."

"Seriously?"

"Remember, you are preaching to the choir. But didn't we just have this conversation?"

I felt like we were always having this exact conversation.

"This felt different. We need to have this conversation and decide what happens at the end of the year. My boss needs to know if I will be back next year."

As the end of 2020 approached, there was no light at the end of the tunnel. Our wishful thinking was hit with the reality that nothing would change. Every week was a new pandemic milestone followed by a new restriction. And a vaccination? They were working on it, but there was no credible timeline provided.

Despite the pandemic and the uncertainty of it all, we had to make decisions now that would affect us nine months later.

We started by asking questions about our situation.

How has our North Star shifted?

What unfinished business did we have?

What did the kids want?

Was this lifestyle sustainable?

What did we know?

For nearly a year, the pandemic has brought endless changes. Yet, we believed we made the right choice to move abroad. Every day has been filled with memorable, once-in-a-lifetime moments that we deeply appreciated. Even the basic routines of getting to school, exploring a new park, or adventures in the grocery store provided experiences that we value.

We knew we could always go back to our home in California. And, if we made that decision, we would settle down and return to our original life permanently. We exerted so much effort and resources to pull off this journey that we had to be certain if we were returning. Returning wasn't bad, but we weren't ready.

Our North Star stayed true. Maricar and I continued to prioritize quality time together and creating memorable experiences for our kids, and we recognized the value of surrounding ourselves with fresh and new environments. Now that we were over a year into this thing, I started to question if it was our surroundings or our circumstances that forced us to have a zestful approach to living our everyday lives.

It was both. We didn't need to be somewhere abroad to have an "adventure is out there" mentality, but it helped.

We operated on a countdown, constantly aware that our window with the children was closing and our time abroad was finite. It was numbered by remaining weeks, weekends, seasons, and holiday breaks. In the past, we often used the "there will be another time" excuse to either postpone or cancel. We were living abroad and now was the time.

Were our golden years of parenting over?

Possibly. The kids were still out of diapers, but were we still the center of their world? Did they still want to hang out with us? Did they have so much attitude now that we didn't want to hang out with them?

When setting out on our initial plan, two years felt like a stretch, and an extension wasn't an option we considered.

We were approaching the teenage years, and we heard horror stories. Jero would be 12 for the next academic year and begin to voice his strong opinions instead of just going with the flow. Not even an official teenager yet, we were getting a healthy occasional dose of "I'm going to disagree with everything my parents say". Lea wasn't far behind.

With high school around the corner, we wanted to provide stability as he navigated deeper friendships beyond our family. We didn't want to take that experience from him or create a parent-child relationship where he would hate us forever.

What's the plan?

We wanted options and decided to cast a wide net with no particular destination. With concrete possibilities, we could weigh the advantages and disadvantages and get the kids involved in the decision-making process.

Returning to California was our safety net since we knew what to expect and could easily transition back if we wanted.

Berlin was a viable option and our default plan. We loved our experience thus far and could see living here for an additional year. There was so much of the country that we hadn't yet explored. However, we had three reservations:

1. The quality of the education at the current school was lacking. It wasn't bad per se, but it wasn't up to our high standards.

2. We were getting by with minimal German, with little to no effort to improve. If we stayed longer, we had to commit and learn the language.

3. Financially, we would be hit with a huge tax bill. Because of a special classification, teachers at JFKS were exempt from taxes for the first two years. If a teacher decided to stay beyond that, they would be taxed at 40%, with the possibility of paying back taxes for the first two years.

The plan was to stay in Berlin unless a better option opened up.

With two years of international secondary math teaching experience and a teacher shortage, Maricar went through the process of applying for positions worldwide starting in October. It seemed like only yesterday that she went through this.

This was a time-intensive load on top of her day job, but Maricar is the type of person who saw the application process like planning our next holiday. Whenever she checked the job board, it was like seeing the recommended travel destinations on Skyscanner. When a school reached back out with a keen interest, it was the equivalent of a vlogger detailing their experience from a recent trip. Like going on holiday, planning a trip was almost as fun as going on the actual trip because you can let your imagination go wild.

Teachers and schools performed this recruiting dance every year. Everyone was making plans early for the next academic year, so they weren't left partnerless when the dance started in the fall.

There were three big hiring pushes:

Fall. If schools knew of vacancies, they started recruiting and would ideally fill these roles before winter break.

Winter. Schools required teachers to decide if they were going to return for the next academic school year by December. This deadline provided the administrative team with a picture of their personnel needs, and they could then fill these positions at the beginning of the calendar year. This was when the bulk of hiring happened.

Spring/Summer. The unexpected happens. A teacher may decide to retire, be away on parental leave, or make a last-minute decision to leave the school. Regardless, schools are still filling roles, and the urgency increases as the first day of school approaches.

What would be ideal?

Take advantage of the fall hiring push and go into the new year with peace of mind and the most significant decision made. If we could pull it off, the next eight months would be a fun "Default to Yes" ride. It would be the equivalent of getting accepted to college and having the next few months dedicated to living it up.

This wasn't the first dance for schools, and they used bonuses and incentives with deadlines to get teachers to be transparent. It forced us to answer the question: Do we roll the dice to find someplace new, or do we play it safe with a confirmed position at our current school? Because of the appeal of the early opportunities and Maricar's stellar teaching track record, we decided to bet on us and see where this journey would lead.

Whenever a viable position caught her eye, she would pitch it back to the family over dinner.

"How about Bogota?" asked Maricar.

"As in Colombia?"

"Here's a video of the school."

"That looks nice. Why is everyone wearing sweaters? Isn't it hot there?" I asked.

"Is it going to be safe? Wasn't Narcos based there?"

"I'd live there. We can explore all of South and Central America. Although, we'd all have to learn Spanish."

"If we live there, we have to go to Antarctica."

"Okay."

"Compensation looks pretty low. Do they cover three kids?"

"No. We'd have to pay that out of pocket."

"That would get pretty expensive."

"Based on the compensation, I would expect the cost of living to be lower."

"What do we have to lose?"

That was always the question. We were playing with house money, and everything had an upside. We were dreamers.

We completed the hard part nearly two years ago when we decided to leave our predetermined path and then actually did it. Now that we were free physically and mentally, few barriers prevented us from moving from one country to another. It was as if we were holding an open plane ticket, and as long as there was a route to a destination, it was fair game.

These were the conversations and hypotheticals we had at our warped blue dinner table for a month.

"How about Maui? Costa Rica? Bangkok? Stuttgart? Amsterdam?"

Our initial logic when evaluating any given city or country wasn't calculated. We based our decisions on what we saw in the media and what our gut told us. For each city, there was at least one deal breaker that made us hesitate.

With Costa Rica, there would be a huge cultural adjustment. The location of the school was far from the beach. The cost of living was high relative to compensation. We would need a car and have to learn the language.

Bangkok? It was a hot and dense city. We weren't city folk.

As for Maui, it was Maui! But the kids would need to attend the local schools and we were concerned that we would feel trapped and get island fever.

With Bogota, the weather was pleasant year-round because of the elevation. We had hesitations about safety and cost of living relative to compensation.

Going through each potential location helped us define what we were looking for.

A great school community. We knew that this was where we would spend most of our time, which was a huge factor in our day-to-day happiness. Is this a school that would bring out our children's best selves and a place they will be excited to go to every day? Could we see the kids completing secondary here? Does the faculty support one another? Does the administration support their employees?

Cost of living vs. compensation. Life was good when you didn't have to worry about money. Moving to a developing country would mean the cost of living and compensation would be lower. You've probably heard the phrase earn dollars, spend pesos. Not only did we want to minimize our daily expenses, but we wanted to have a financial buffer so we could travel freely.

Location and accessibility. We came to appreciate safety and wanted the kids to be able to wander the neighborhood. It also had to be centrally located, making travel easy. In a post-pandemic world, we would take advantage of every opportunity.

Every time Maricar had an interview, which seemed like twice a week, we would play "library" quietly in the hallway. It was more of a mudroom, and we'd sit on the stairs or the floor.

Maricar asserted, "I got an interview in ten minutes. That means you have five minutes to grab whatever you need."

The four of us would then silently squish together, often reading a book because we'd get too loud in any competitive card game. No discernable answers made it through the thick door, but we could at least tell when she finished.

I was the adult in the room, and not laughing was hard. It was like when my parents would drag my brothers and me to church. The silence would make me think about the funniest parts of my day. To hold back my giggles, I would have to pinch myself as a distraction, and by communion, I'd have red nail indentations on the back of my hands.

Eventually, Maricar would open the door to let us back into the room, and we could all speak normally again. This routine was most challenging for Jero, who always seemed to have something he needed to say.

What About Hong Kong?

Schools know what they are looking for and move quickly when the right teacher comes along. It took less than a week from submitting an application to getting an offer from Discovery College.

Maricar had never been to Hong Kong, and I visited once when I was five on a Cathay Pacific stopover to the Philippines. We never considered it a destination. What made Discovery College attractive?

The International Baccalaureate Program, test scores, and focus on the child's holistic development would be great for the kids. Their education was and continued to be a high priority.

The school was a proper international institution with all the bells and whistles. It was part of the English Schools Foundation (ESF) and was a massive step up compared to the facilities and resources at JFKS. These weren't a necessity, but since they came with the package, we might as well enjoy them.

The tenure and experience of the staff seemed attractive as it looked like many teachers stayed on for years. After being a part of several school communities and having the inside scoop on most of them because of Maricar's connections, we knew teacher engagement mattered. If teachers aren't supported, they will invest mediocre effort and leave.

Lastly, the school was in Discovery Bay. This is not what we imagined Hong Kong to be. It was a densely packed suburb isolated from the rest of the world by a mountain range and the sea. Private cars were prohibited, so people got around by walking, taking a bus, or using a golf cart.

It was a holiday resort and only a 30-minute ferry ride from Central. People would go here on the weekends to escape the city. This place was also a hotspot neighborhood for pilots and crew, which told us everything we needed to know about its strategic location.

There were two international schools, two central beaches, and two plazas at either end of the 2.5 square mile lush oasis.

This place couldn't be real.

Apart from being in the middle of Southeast Asia, we knew that Hong Kong was dense and expensive. The pleasant surprise was learning about the amount of nature, miles of trails, and the accessibility of it all.

On paper, everything checked out, even the finances. It would be tight, but we knew from experience we could make it work by mercilessly cutting expenses that weren't essential.

What did the kids have to say?

We planted the seed that Berlin would be temporary, and although they each built solid friendships and would be happy to stay, there was no resistance.

The international community was transient, and people learned to go with the flow. Nothing was permanent, and when it comes to people, you must be ready to say goodbye to friends and make new ones.

Our advantage was that we always moved as a family, which provided a buffer to the changes around us.

For those who have lived this lifestyle for a while, it was easier to be the one leaving than staying. With the former, a new world was ahead with so many changes that it keeps the mind active. In contrast, when staying behind, a new normal has to be established, while being reminded constantly of how things used to be.

Discovery College marketed as a Tier 1 university. They knew how to package their offerings in a way that would entice anyone.

With this as supporting material, it made the sale to the kids easy.

"This is where we are going? Wow!" Feris said.

The other thing they cared about was where we were going to live.

We set the bar by telling them that Hong Kong was one of the most expensive cities in the world and apartments were small. We showed examples of cage apartments where people would have a communal area and a personal space that could only accommodate a bed. We may have taken things too far.

We had the advantage of knowing that anything would be a step up from our one room and assured the kids they would participate in the apartment search and decision-making.

The most important conversation was with Jero. He just turned eleven, was easygoing, and already looking forward to the change, yet uncertain what this would mean for him. We played out various potential scenarios of how long we would be in this new community and how that might affect his choices.

For example, if we left before he started high school, he would be able to start as a freshman in the US. Alternatively, if things went well, there was the potential of finishing high school abroad. We would take it one year at a time, checking in with one another to affirm if we were still on the right path.

There were no guarantees of what would happen, but I hoped he appreciated that we took him aside for this grown-up conversation.

As people age, they establish routines, settle into what is comfortable, and resist change. How much stability was necessary as a baseline to continue living the "experience-first" lifestyle we had constructed?

This pandemic was still raging in the background of our decisions, and it seemed to only be getting worse. How did we factor in this card?

This too shall pass. Despite another wave in the fall and winter, we were hopeful about the prospects of a vaccine, effective safety measures, and the virus's negative correlation with warmer weather. We didn't bother researching the virus because we were utterly convinced that next year, everything would improve, and the world would be a better place.

Maricar accepted the position, and we shifted our focus to making the most of our remaining six months in Europe. We were in a positive mindset, viewing the world through rose-tinted glasses.

Our goal was to play our hand wisely, ensuring no regrets when we left in July.

In Their Words:
What's Next?

Jero (11):

- *I didn't know much about Hong Kong. The website with pictures and a pool impressed me. Almost like a private island. A beach resort. It had the holiday look of a tropical getaway like Cancun.*
- *Mommy was doing interviews with different schools like Costa Rica, and I would get excited hearing about all these places. Most didn't work because they were cut off from the rest of the world or too expensive compared to the salary.*
- *I remember when she had her interview. It was at a time when I was learning how to play crazy train. I was excited to hear how the interview went and show her what I learned.*

Lea (9):

- *I didn't really care where we went next because it didn't seem like a big deal. I don't even remember being told we were going to Hong Kong. That shows how much it mattered to me.*
- *I remember thinking it would be a warmer version of Germany except with beaches. I got the idea because my friend's mom went to Hong Kong, and that's what she said.*

- *I remember my Zoom interview where someone from the school asked me a whole bunch of questions and even had to do a show and tell. I wasn't nervous about the interview, but I wanted to get it over with. What's the worst that could happen? They wouldn't let me go to school?*

Feris (6):

- *I thought Hong Kong would be like Berlin except more city-like. I wanted to stay in Berlin because it snows, and I liked the Korean restaurant.*

18

WE PROBABLY SHOULDN'T, BUT WE DID

Rome, December 2020 (Week 74)

This would be our last Christmas in Germany, and the Christmas markets weren't happening. Well, that sucked.

COVID numbers were rising, and the government was shutting everything down to slow the virus.

We understood the situation but didn't want to spend our last winter break in the basement. We had the itch to go somewhere, anywhere.

Our apartment was warm and clean. It gave us reliable Wi-Fi, utilities, and a roof, but it was just uncomfortable enough that we wanted to get out.

Our pandemic travel conversations were now routine.

"What are our options?" I asked.

"Rome!" Maricar proposed.

"Really? Rome for Christmas? Mass at the Vatican? That would be pretty cool."

"It's not going to be easy."

"What do you mean?"

"Testing. Paperwork. Quarantine. Potentially getting stuck. And we don't know if things are necessarily better there."

"If it's doable, then I don't care. I feel trapped and spending the holidays in this box would be the worst. Even if we traveled to Rome and got stuck in an Airbnb, it would be ten times better than this. What do we have to do?"

"Specialized testing is the new normal. It has to be administered at specific facilities and completed within a 48-hour window before a flight. Results are generally available within 24 hours."

Beyond the cost of 50 euros a pop, the process was inconvenient. There was also limited information on where or how to take a test. It was either brilliant or stupid by design: they would make it so difficult to travel that people would weed themselves out because they would give up trying.

On our first attempt, we took a 75-minute bus ride to the brand-new, nine years behind schedule, Berlin Brandenburg Airport. Getting there was an ordeal because the travel infrastructure to the airport didn't yet exist.

Rumors were that tests were limited, and it was first come first serve. We played it safe by blocking out a whole evening and then timed our arrival for when it was least crowded.

We arrived and were greeted by a line snaking outside the airport. There were only a few places to get tested in Berlin and with the Christmas holidays approaching, this was the place to be. To make things worse, it was mid-December, so not only did it get dark at 4 p.m., but it was cold. We were expecting at least three hours of this misery.

The bright lights of the airport and the people in the long line entertained the kids. They were happy to get off the bus and move around. I tried to stay positive as I thought about spending Christmas in Rome.

Thirty minutes into our wait in the slowly creeping line, a representative came out and began providing updates to the people in front. I hoped she would bring good news. She worked her way back to where we stood.

The good news was that we didn't have to stand in line any longer. The bad news was that we missed the cut-off based on the length of the line and how many tests they could administer before closing.

Jero asked. "So, can we go home now?"

"Yes." I answered.

"Why?"

"They close at 9 p.m., and they only have enough time to test another 100 people. We didn't make the cut."

"Can we get something to eat on the way back? I think I saw a currywurst place."

"Okay. I'm hungry, too."

Returning unsuccessful was frustrating. It was a colossal waste of time, and we had to return the next day. There were no shortcuts, and it was the travel tax that everyone had to pay. We were clear about what we wanted and accepted the situation. Fortunately, our flight wasn't until Friday, and we still had a day to get tested. It also meant that it was our last chance, or this trip would be a no-go.

Immediately after school the next day, we repeated the process. This time, we arrived five hours before closing, wore extra layers, and brought a bag full of snacks. We were ready for whatever they threw at us. The line looked as long as it did yesterday, but we thought *it could be worse.*

Like yesterday, a representative came out 30 minutes into our wait and worked their way from the front of the line to the back. Déjà vu. I thought we came early enough to make the cut. Looking ahead, he was pulling people out of line randomly. For what, I don't know.

He got to us, sized us up, and started asking questions in German.

"Wie viele Personen in Ihrer Familie?"

"Es tut mir Leid. Englisch, bitte."

"How many people in your group?"

"Five."

"Okay, please come with me."

"Where are we going?" ask Feris.

"I don't know. Whatever it is, I think it's a good thing."

He then led us inside and into a separate line with only a handful of people who either had elderly or small children. Our three-hour wait was cut to less than an hour. I love Germany.

They tested us, and we went home. We would be back for a third day in a row to catch our flight. Well, that would be the case if we tested negative.

Walking through the airport and knowing what we had to do to travel made the whole experience sweeter.

Luckily, all the tests were negative, and our paperwork was accepted. Because of previous experiences and the fact that our feelings of rejection were still fresh, we didn't take any of it for granted.

Once in Rome and on the way to our Airbnb from the Leonardo da Vinci–Fiumicino Airport, we listened to the news on the radio.

Here were the headlines:

"Because of increasing positive cases, Italy is going into lockdown for 3-5 days before, during, and after Christmas."

"Travel between states is restricted."

"The Vatican and Rome curfews will continue."

"All public celebrations have been canceled."

"All tourists need to carry paperwork with them at all times."

If we had flown out a day later, would we even have been able to get into the country? We were in Rome for less than an hour, and I'm questioning whether we should even be here.

At this rate, who knew if we could even step outside tomorrow? We had to take advantage now.

"It's still before curfew, let's go for a walk," said Maricar.

I asked. "Where are we going to go?"

"Doesn't matter. This is Rome and we are bound to see something historic."

It was 7 p.m. on a Friday, and the streets were a ghost town as we wandered and enjoyed the slightly warmer temperatures. By now, the kids were used to wandering with no destination. We ended up at the Pantheon and then Trevi Fountain. To help us understand the significance of these iconic landmarks, we would watch a little Rick Steves' Ancient Rome when we returned to our room.

For Maricar and I, it felt like we were just here. And we were, just two years ago, when the wheels started turning, imagining this life.

All I needed was that walk to help put my mind at ease. We made the right decision to come here. Even if everything were closed, and we spent our days walking the streets and our nights watching Netflix with home-cooked meals, it would be all worth it.

In seven months, we would be in Hong Kong. It was on the other side of the world, about as far as San Francisco is from Berlin. Besides Maricar's teaching position and knowing we would be moving there in July, we didn't have much else planned. Our focus now was on the European countdown amid the global pandemic—a dangerous combination. Our canned response to any invitation or idea would be:

"Let's do it."

"Why not?"

"Yes!"

As we were in a state of bliss, I received an email from our landlord, who knew something was up despite our limited daily contact. She monitored us through the Strava app, where I posted all my runs and walks. It said:

> **"We see that you are in Rome. It's irresponsible given the current world pandemic. This act shows that we have different priorities. If you decide to continue to behave this way, you'll need to find another place to live."**

I understood. We followed the rules, but there were unsaid ones about how we should behave in the middle of a pandemic. Unlike the American mentality of what was best for the individual, Germans focused on what was best for the community.

Additionally, they were not willing to incur unnecessary risks. They were thinking about their family's safety. We were a liability.

Our approach was about taking calculated risks and precautions, but we also recognized that what we were doing differed from what most people would be comfortable with.

Rather than share our reasons, which they could interpret as excuses, we said they were right and that we would play by their rules moving forward. I learned early as a kid that sometimes, it was best to bite my tongue and not add to the fire.

We knew why we wanted what we wanted.

Our regular living conditions consisted of a basement-level room. Because of the size, it afforded minimal privacy and individual space. It met our basic needs, but we wanted to spend as little time there as possible.

A proper German staycation was not an option. The country was on lockdown, and overnight travel between German states was off-limits, but it was okay to travel internationally.

Berlin winter weather sucked. The sun rose late and set early. It was always overcast, wet, and cold, but not cold enough for real snow. The lively atmosphere of the *Weihnachtsmarkt* helped with the gloom, but this year, there were none.

Our time was limited, and we wanted to make every day count. We traveled responsibly and avoided crowds. And due to Rome's restrictions at the time, in our minds, it would be the same if not similar to Berlin's safety protocols.

Rome was glorious.

I took the time to explore early every morning. Regardless of when I went to bed, I jumped awake excited about where I would run each morning. The Coliseum one day, the Vatican another, speed work along the Tiber River, intervals on the Spanish Steps, and then repeat it all. It was heaven.

During the day, places were open for lunch, and although most of the city would shut down after 6 p.m., we got a pretty typical Roman holiday except without the crowds and heat. The other benefit was that we could take our time because many tourist places were closed.

We had low expectations, no agenda, and savored exploring. Rather than cram two weeks of activities into one, we divided one week into two. That was a luxury, especially for the kids who saw the activities as things they had to endure before they could lounge at home in front of a screen.

One of the best experiences was being in the vast St. Peter's Square for Christmas. There was no Midnight Mass that year, but the decorations, including the centerpiece Christmas tree, pulled everything together. It got us into the spirit.

We returned to Berlin a day before New Year's Eve and went straight into a three-day self-regulated quarantine in our one-room apartment. Nothing physically kept us in, but this is Germany, and there were eyes everywhere. You could feel them behind every window.

We planned ahead by stocking up on food and ordered Monopoly. Our New Year's Eve, or Saint Sylvester's Day, was spent in our basement apartment. We heard the fireworks going off well until 2 a.m., and now and then, we would glimpse fireworks that would shine in the open sliver between houses.

Quarantine gave us time to think about our living situation. The basement was supposed to be a band-aid, but here we were, months beyond our projected timeframe. How were we still here? It was like being in a bad relationship, constantly forgiving your partner, thinking it would improve. The next thing you know, it's 20 years later, and you wonder why you are still in it. Or, on a more positive note, it's running a marathon telling your body to get to the next mile, and after doing that enough, you are surprised when the end is in sight.

We saw the finish line approaching and decided we would grind this out. We were doing okay, and there was enough change in the world that we didn't want to introduce more.

"Was it worth it?" I asked.

"You mean Rome?" Maricar clarified.

"Yeah, the risk, the quarantine, and even missing our last German New Year's Eve?"

"Absolutely, and I'd do it again in a heartbeat," Maricar replied confidently.

"Just wanted to make sure we're on the same page," I said seeking reassurance.

We rang in the New Year in quarantine, feeling cautiously optimistic about 2021. We were eager to explore Europe as much as possible, but wondered if that would even be feasible.

Would things continue to deteriorate before improving?

And how would our risk tolerance hold up under the strain?

Uncertainty loomed, but we remained hopeful.

In Their Words:
Rome

Jero (11):

- *One of my favorite places. When we traveled, we always had an itinerary where we would do so many things. This was different. We stayed for nearly two weeks, and we took our time.*
- *Mommy and I went for a run on Christmas Day and went to where the bishop stays. That was nice.*
- *We ate so much food. Everything from fancy places to a hole in the street. We kept getting gelato. The tiramisu and pesto were good. There was a place with a good selection of meats and breads. Prosciutto or something.*
- *At one point, we didn't go outside at all. To get exercise, we did Tae Bo using videos on YouTube.*

Lea (9):

- *Really good food everywhere we went. I remember this pasta place that had pesto and regular* [marinara] pasta. *Best ever. The pizza we got was also really good. And the desserts, especially the tiramisu from a place called Roma something—so good.*
- *When there, I learned that the Vatican is its own country. The one bad meal was when we had horse poop pasta* [Note from

James: She is referencing cacio e pepe]. *It smelled and tasted like horse poop. You know how you can tell the taste of something by the smell? This is an example of that. Looked yummy, tasted awful.*

- *Walked through a lot of cobblestone streets. They were clean and vintage-looking. Both old and new at the same time.*

Feris (6):

- *I remember a nice water fountain with a man.*
- *Got Kiki for Christmas. Kiki is my stuffed grey and white Koala. Really fluffy and about the size of my hands. It came with a box with a window that is its home. Every Christmas, we get something for each other. We have a rotation. This year, Kuya Jero got me.*
- *We visited the Colosseum, and I wanted to climb it. It looked like it was hit by a big boulder.*

19
PLAYING BY THE RULES

Berlin, February 2021 (Week 83)

Maricar asked me one day, "We are running out of time. Should we try to go somewhere for *Winterferien*, winter break?"

"I don't think so. Numbers are too high, and we are being watched by you-know-who. Even if we did go, is there even a place we could go?"

"Fingers crossed that things get better soon. I'm going to put together a travel wish list."

"Good idea. What's going to be first?"

"Iceland."

"Really? You do know that while things are warming up in Berlin, we would be going to a place that is even colder? Is it just because Justin Bieber and every celebrity is making it famous on IG?"

"No. It's going to be amazing, and I want to see the Northern Lights."

"You are thinking big. I could just show you a picture of the Northern Lights."

"Stop it."

"What's it going to cost us? Are there any restrictions?"

"It will be expensive no matter what we do, and we'll have to jump through a lot of hoops. But Iceland is one of the safest places with regards to the virus."

"Sure. Let's do it. It will give us something to plan and keep us busy during the winter. Do you think any of our friends would be crazy enough to go?"

"I have an idea and I'll go ask them."

"In the meantime, my friend has a sled that we could borrow."

"That sounds fun."

It was a long stretch from January to March 2021, but it didn't feel like we were missing anything. The pandemic was so bad that we didn't even have the option to travel. It was about accepting and making the most of the situation in times like these. We've had a lot of opportunities since leaving 18 months ago to practice this mentality.

I look back at my Strava runs during this period, and my descriptions always included the words dark and cold. My body adapted, and I got used to the conditions. Once it got below freezing, it didn't matter much anymore. It was just cold. Unless I was injured, I would run every day. The only time I would think twice was when it was sleeting, the nasty in-between where it's cold, wet, and the ground is slush. It was the worst because you would get wet from the slushy mixture, and it was only a matter of time before the cold took hold.

Maybe it was my fault. As Germans like to say, *"Es gibt kein schlechtes Wetter, nur schlechte Kleidung."* "There is no bad weather, just bad clothing."

A week of relentless snowfall transformed Berlin into a magical winter wonderland, providing a much-needed respite from monotony. The kids reveled in the rare treat, playing outside every day, savoring the moment without knowing when it would end.

Then, in a sudden turn, warmth arrived, and everyone's spirits lifted, strides lengthened. Surviving the long winter made spring's arrival doubly sweet.

In Their Words:
Berlin Snow

Jero (11):

- *Berlin usually has a cold and muddy feeling. The snow changed everything up. It made it Christmas-y, like a whole new place to explore. When it snowed, it was a big deal because it hadn't happened in years.*
- *I remember sledding with my friends. There was a hill in front of our school that I would usually bike down. It turned into a sledding place where Felix, Campbell, and I would go down. Looking back, I see it was dangerous because there were trees and roots in the way.*
- *We also visited a place where the river froze over. It was so big that it felt like the ocean. Boats were stuck, and you could walk right up to them. At one point, I heard the ice cracking, so I ran to the shore.*

Lea (9):

- *Started as misty snow, then I remembered telling Daddy to quickly get my snow stuff out of storage because I was afraid it was all going to melt.*
- *It kept snowing, and we went to a nearby apartment complex*

with lots of grass. Snow was mixed with mud, but it was okay because we were able to make a snowman.

- *It continued to snow. I borrowed a sled and went down the hill at the* park [Schönower Park] *next to the school and the one with the long hill* [Fischtalpark]. *The pond froze over, and we dared one another to walk across. It was one of the best times to be in Berlin.*
- *So cold my hands would freeze. I never had the right size gloves. They would always be too big, so that I wouldn't wear them. When I got to school, my hands would be frozen and itchy.*

Feris (6):

- *Feris doesn't remember this part of the adventure. At the time, she loved making snow angels, rolling snow into a giant ball and riding the sled down a hill with someone, never alone.*

20

HARDLY SURVIVING THE LAND OF FIRE AND ICE

Iceland, April 2021 (Week 91)

As per routine, Maricar and I walked through our travel checklist.

"A blessing from our landlord?" I asked.

"Check," said Maricar.

"Now that's out of the way, what else do we have to do?"

"Book a quarantine hotel. Book a camper van. Map out the route."

Traveling to Iceland was challenging because of the pandemic measures that were put in place to keep the virus out. It was next level.

Hurdle #1—Testing

In addition to the usual testing, there was testing on arrival. Even if we tested negative, if someone in our same row or the row in front or behind us tested positive, we would have to go into an extended quarantine at our own cost.

"Really? So, you are telling me we could spend our whole Iceland trip in quarantine?" I asked Maricar.

"Yup. So, we need to strategically choose our seats, ensuring we are around the fewest people possible. I'm thinking the back left corner."

"Works for me."

Hurdle #2—Quarantine

Regardless of our test results, we would be in quarantine for a minimum of three days. We weren't allowed to go outside or even get groceries.

"So, for our Iceland trip, we can expect to spend at least 20% of it in quarantine? How are we supposed to get food?" Maricar was used to my endless questions at this point.

"If we get a place that is away from the city and there isn't a risk of coming into contact with anyone, then we can go outside for a walk," answered Maricar.

"And, what about food?"

"We would have to arrange for someone to deliver this to us. "

"Those places and services exist?"

"Because of these new rules and people that are desperate enough to visit, they exist now."

"Okay. I guess someone is always finding new ways to make money. I'll find a place."

Hurdle #3—Testing Again

"And finally, if we make it past the initial test and get through quarantine," said Maricar, "we have a final test that we need to take before we can go anywhere."

"So, you are telling me we could potentially sit around on our fourth day, just waiting for our results to come back. And if they are positive, we could go straight back to quarantine? That would suck a lot. It's like getting out of detention, tasting freedom, only to be called back because of something you say on the way out."

Hurdle #4—Testing Again and Again

"Before we could fly back to Germany, we would need to get tested again at least 24 hours before our flight, meaning we had to be in Reykjavik early. Then, we would have to quarantine again when we arrive in Berlin."

"And you want to go through all this so that we can say we saw the Northern Lights?" I asked.

"About that: I did some research, and seeing the Northern Lights, especially at this time of the season, isn't likely because of the cloud cover," said Maricar.

"Okay. So, you are telling me there is a chance, but we should set low expectations and hope for the best. Got it."

Iceland was not expecting many visitors.

Maricar likes to think big, and she is stubbornly committed when she decides on a goal or task. Because this is something that she wanted to do, and we were going big, I barely flinched as she filled me in on all the risks. It highlighted what mattered and showed what we would do to get it.

In addition to the hoops we had to jump through to be able to travel in Iceland, we were traveling at the beginning of spring, when the snow was beginning to melt, and the weather was highly unpredictable. Some days, people could get away with just two layers in the morning, but by afternoon, the blizzard and intense gusts of wind would trap them indoors.

To give you an idea of how serious the weather can be, we had a mandatory tutorial before they let us check out the van. The two most relevant warnings pertained to the wind: 1) Park facing the wind, and 2) Always open and hold the door with two hands. This would ensure the doors wouldn't blow off the car.

I thought it was an exaggeration until I had to get into the van. Even when I was following protocol, I felt like I was holding on to dear life. Can you imagine the setback if our door got blown off in the middle of Iceland?

If we cleared quarantine—and that was a big if—the plan was to make a counterclockwise loop around Iceland in about a week. Our break was two weeks, but we needed a buffer upon arrival and departure because of pandemic measures.

And what was there to do? Hike and explore the most iconic sites and camp at different places around the island.

A sense of urgency to do it all, limited time, and unpredictable conditions were a dangerous combination.

How aggressive was the pace? On the last day of our three-day quarantine, we drove to Reykjavik to get tested as soon as the facility opened. Then, we spent five hours hiking to, from, and around an actively erupting Fagradalsfjall volcano. If that wasn't enough, we finished with a five-mile Reykjadalur hot spring thermal river hike that took nearly three hours because of the elevation and icy conditions. An extended twilight till about 9 p.m. ensured we weren't walking in the dark. That was the first day.

I drove and kept us fed while Maricar, the brains of the operation, mapped out the places to visit, places to stay and kept us on schedule.

I was always thinking about the food plan. It has been my thing since I was little. I would easily and regularly get hangry and liked to have food around. I had the kids eat beforehand and bring a snack wherever we went, knowing they needed fuel for our adventures.

Nothing grows in Iceland, so everything has to be imported, driving up the costs of everyday things, including food. Our luggage was half winter clothes and half food supplies to cut costs.

Eating out wasn't an option. The restaurants were either closed, out of our budget or non-existent. Our meals, cooked in a camper van, consisted of instant ramen, oatmeal, a Spam knock-off, canned chicken, green bananas, pasta, bread, peanut butter, jelly, packaged pasta, and IKEA chocolate bars. I brought at least a dozen bars, which helped satisfy our sweet tooth and provided a pick-me-up on the trails. I always had one and was ready to dish out a square when energy or morale was low.

Our CampEasy Campervan was the Easy Big X. The company described it as "The Family Choice," and it could accommodate five with a small top loft and a bottom "full living room" that converted into a bed. There was a sink, cooler fridge, small stove, and table. It got the job done.

Cooking inside the van was challenging. The layout resembled a restaurant dining booth, which made meals very communal. Between the passenger seats and the front was our "kitchen." Most items were easy to prepare as they were already precooked and needed either rehydration or to be warmed up. The staple that gave me the most trouble was pasta. The water never boiled, extending the usual cooking time from ten to 30 minutes. I practically gave up on it.

"What does everyone want for dinner tonight? We can have ramen or mystery meat."

"Ramen!" everybody chimed in.

Our diet for the trip wasn't the healthiest or tastiest, but it was enough to keep our bellies full and gave us the energy for long, hike-filled days.

Each night, we slept in an ice chest. The overnight heater in our camper didn't work properly—that, or I couldn't figure it out—so we bundled up every night. We wore layers, huddled up for body warmth, and put on thick duvet blankets over our heads to trap in the heat. In the morning, ice was coating the inside of the van and our bananas changed from dark green to black. If you exposed a limb outside the sheets, you would wake up because it got too cold.

It had to be an emergency if you wanted to use the bathroom at night.

"Daddy, I need to use the bathroom," said Feris.

"Are you sure you have to?"

"Yeah. I really have to go."

"Fine. Let me know when you have your jacket and shoes on, and then I'll follow."

"I need help putting on my shoes."

"Okay."

Regardless of the time, using the bathroom required bundling up and a short walk. It was fine when we got outside, but it was logistically painful.

"Ready?"

"Yes."

"Here we go."

Once we opened the sliding door, snow would enter, and the van temperature would drop from cold to colder. Anything the snow touched would eventually melt, making it damp. It only took one midnight bathroom experience to teach them to use it before bed or to hold it.

Each day consisted of driving for a few hours, setting up or breaking down camp, hiking, and exploring. We were often braving the elements or cruising around in our van. We didn't bring much and wore the same thing. We each had a set for sleeping and another for the day. The only thing that would change would be our underwear.

Maricar and I stuck to our morning running routine, so our gear would often hang in the van throughout the day to dry. To be honest, our clothes never quite dried. They were always damp from the elements outside or from condensation. The most reliable drying method was to either put them on, stand in the sun if it was out, or put them on the vent while we were driving. As you can imagine, the vents were prime spots because everyone wanted at least dry socks and shoes. The cold controlled all smells, but after the third day on the road, there was a mellow but persistent mildew smell.

On day four of post-quarantine, we started with an early search for a secret natural hot tub, the Djúpavogskörin Hot Springs. We got there early and had the place to ourselves. It was not visible from the road and required a short hike, but it was beautiful once you arrived. It was relaxing with 360 views of the sea, coastline, and mountains.

Finding it and getting in was the easy part. This was the warmest and most comfortable we had been on the whole trip. The problem was leaving. It was as if there was a spell holding you back. And as soon as you exposed a limb out of the water, an icy gust would tell you to go back in.

Maricar, ever the timekeeper, eventually compelled us out. And get out we did because it would have been better to face the wrath of Iceland's elements than to not listen to Maricar.

The rest of the day included minimal stops and scenic driving as we went from the southern part of the island and through an overpass to the other side. Our midpoint was the Stuðlagil Canyon Viewpoint, where we experienced the coldest temperatures of our lives at negative 24 degrees Fahrenheit. We should have interpreted the cold as a bad omen for things to come.

A blizzard hit as we made our way through the overpass on Highway 1. We were too far in by this point, and there were no rest stops close behind or ahead, so we decided to push through. Conditions continued to get worse to the point of whiteout. As a Californian, these conditions were new to me. There was so much snow blowing that the road became nearly invisible, matching the snow-covered landscape. I could barely see a meter in any direction.

"Is there anything in the road that I might hit?"

"Am I still on the road?"

"Is there a car on the other side of this two-lane highway?"

"What happens if I veer off the road? Is there a ditch? A cliff?"

Because of the nature of the conditions, visibility would change rapidly. One minute, I couldn't see anything, and then, for a window of three seconds, I could see ten meters ahead, giving me confidence that the road was straight. It wreaked havoc on my anxiety, never providing a moment to relax.

My experience with long runs helped. I was used to chunking out longer runs into manageable pieces and focusing on progress and little wins. This drive was about finding and getting to the next road delineator because the snow erased the road and the pavement markers. I knew I was on the road as long as I kept the markers on my side. From marker to marker, there would be a few seconds where I couldn't see anything. And in these moments, I would hold my breath.

You might ask, "Why not just stop the car or pull over?"

We explored that option countless times. For one, we didn't have service in the mountains and didn't know how far we had to go or if the conditions would change at any point. Secondly, visibility was so bad that we feared another car would eventually hit us from behind if we stopped. Third, for the duration of the drive, we looked for a place to pull off the road. There were no margins or turnoffs. We were in the wrong stretch at the wrong time.

Our best option was to push ahead cautiously.

There were times when I thought this was the end. My fear of driving off the road and over a cliff or getting stuck in this weather overwhelmed me and kept me on high alert. I never let down my guard, completely focused on getting to the next marker and keeping my eyes peeled for all the information I could gather from the ever-changing landscape.

"Daddy, are we there yet?" asked Lea.

"Don't talk to me. Maricar?"

"No, we aren't there. This will probably take a while."

"Is everything okay?"

"Yup. Just taking it slow."

After three nerve-wracking hours white-knuckling the steering wheel, I was mentally and physically exhausted. Then came the first sign of life: lights.

"Is that a building we are approaching?"

They were too big to be a vehicle, but then they continued to approach us. It stopped and turned out to be a snowplow. The tension in my shoulders lifted, and we were saved.

A guy in a sleeveless shirt came out of the plow and walked up to our window. After looking over his relaxed attire and nonchalant demeanor, I grinned. I might just be overreacting to the weather. Everything is fine. He told me the road ahead was clear, and I needed to back up so he could get through.

This was the best news I've heard all day and the first time I've smiled in hours.

Crunch.

As I backed up, I bumped into a sign, and it took off my right taillight. I gave Maricar a look, and she gave me a look back that said she was not getting out of the car to help me. I adjusted blindly since visibility was still limited by snow, and it was now dark. I eventually made room, and I imagined the snowplow driver mumbling under his breath, "Tourists."

A broken taillight? If that was all it was, I would take it.

It was getting dark at this point, and I set my sights forward and slowly approached the bridge.

"What bridge? I don't see anything. Do you see it?"

I crept closer to the edge. I feared that with a bridge, there had to be a drop-off on both sides. What if we made it all this way, only to drive off an edge and into freezing water? What then? I continued to creep closer as the bridge's shape slowly revealed itself in the dark. We benefited from the newly plowed roads, and I could sense we were in the home stretch. I aimed to get to the campsite before it got completely dark.

We got to the campsite and were greeted by others taking shelter from the extreme weather. Sharing our near-death experiences connected everyone quickly. We were all in the same boat. It was comforting to hear from others who understood exactly what we had just experienced and could empathize with us. Sometimes, that's all we need—to be heard and understood.

From here, we were halfway through the island road trip, and other than the blizzard, things were going to plan. We even got a few days of clear skies and good weather. This whole experience was uniquely different to anything we had done before. Everything was extreme, including the raw beauty, dangers of nature, and the logistics we had to figure out to make it all happen.

We completed the loop and returned to Reykjavik ahead of schedule.

As with every experience, I turned to Maricar for validation.

"Was it worth it?"

Without hesitation, she said, "yes."

And guess what? We ended up seeing the Northern Lights. Well, Maricar and I saw it. The kids slept through it.

Lessons we learned:

The bad stuff wasn't that bad. After some time and distance, they made for the best stories. The processed food, icy sleeping conditions, sporadic showers, having to wear the same thing, and extremely cold temperatures—it made things interesting. It is the stuff we reference most when we reflect on Iceland and then we shake our heads in disbelief before laughing.

Feris' favorite part of the trip was quarantine. "You don't need to go to Iceland to have an adventure. It's all mental." Feris reminded me of that. So many of her memories are before the adventure started. It's like when the box packaging brings more joy than the toy inside. Is it possible to recreate that joy or does it come spontaneously?

The obstacles added much-needed flavor and made the experience memorable. If we didn't have them, it would be the same story with the same recreated photos on social media. The unexpected detours made it our one-of-a-kind adventure.

After enduring and surviving this, I'd be surprised to find a family adventure we couldn't handle. We had a new sense of confidence that widened our scope of what was doable.

Upon returning to Berlin, the city was bursting with life as flowers bloomed and trees donned vibrant green foliage. With each passing week, the temperature steadily rose, ushering in a sense of renewal.

With just a few months remaining, it was time to shed our winter layers and embrace the lightness of warmer days. I was more than ready to bid farewell to snow, and the thought of Hong Kong's balmy climate became increasingly alluring.

In Their Words:
Iceland

Jero (11):

- *Lots of cool things to see and explore, like a giant staircase that led into a crater or a lava tunnel and trails through cool landscapes.*
- *We were driving around the island and had different campsites to get to before it got dark. This limited window meant that we sometimes had to rush, or we could get stuck in the middle of nowhere. One time was the basalt columns. We had to do a hike to see a cave entrance. When we got there, it was already six. Because it was getting dark, we had to rush back to our van.*
- *This is definitely one of my top three favorite vacations.*

Lea (9):

- *It was cold, and we saw a lot of Iceland-y things: A volcano was blowing up close. We hiked up a mountain, even though there wasn't even a trail.*
- *There was a long drive where we got into a small accident and broke the taillight. Afterward, we met a lot of people at the campsite. There was a common area and tables everywhere. Some of the people were two funny Germans, a family of three with a small kid, and the Steeles. Everyone was hanging out*

and talking about stuff. Not crowded, just us. Really cool place.

- *The CampEasy Campervan would get really cold. When the heater was on, water droplets would form. When we turned it off, they would freeze and drop.*

Feris (6):

- *We hiked to the volcano, and it was muddy on the way, so I stepped on the plants.*
- *We went into a hot tub in the wilderness. We would dunk our heads into the water, and when we took it out, frost started to form on our hair because it was so cold.*
- *We stayed in a cabin with a hot tub and video games. There was a songbook that had lyrics and chords that we would sing. "We Built This City" was one of them. There was a frozen stream nearby, and we would take the ice from it, put it into the hot tub, and watch what happened.*
- *When we went into the van, it was so cold. Sometimes, when I'm really hot in Hong Kong, I think about that van.*
- *We went to a hot spring river but got there so late that we didn't go into the water and had to turn back. We went a second time, but this time with the Steeles, and we got to swim in the hot spring. There was a lot of algae in the water, and it was slippery. There were lots of other people there, and it felt weird. It was like showering with them. When it was time to go, and I had to get out. It was so cold.*
- *I really didn't like the campsites because the showers were dirty.*

Some places were nicer than others. I always wanted to see pictures of the campsites before we arrived, so I knew what to expect. Was it clean? Was it nice? Did it have a view?

- *When we would arrive late, I hated showering. I asked Mommy if I could just use baby wipes instead.*

21

THIS TIME, IT'S NOT MY FAULT

Mallorca, June 2021 (Week 97)

With all the long holidays over for the school year, we extended a three-day weekend by pulling a Ferris Bueller and planned a trip to Mallorca, Spain.

- Paperwork triple-checked?
- Testing 36 hours before a flight?
- Checked-in to flight?
- Carry-on baggage meets requirements?
- Double-checked travel requirements?
- Airport transportation?

At this point in our travels, we had missed something on the list at least once, and it caused unnecessary stress, delays, and even a canceled trip. Getting burned once was plenty, and I was determined not to let it happen again. But this time, I swear it was not my fault.

The standard testing requirement to fly is a PCR Test taken within 48 hours of a flight.

Results are available within 24 hours, which means there was a 24-hour window to get tested and still have results on time. Sometimes, flights got delayed or canceled, so it was better to have a buffer and time the test, so it was as close to the flight as possible but far enough that results came in on time.

Thirty hours before our flight and right after school, we went to Mitte [central Berlin] to get tested at a new pop-up facility. We paid 39 euros per person, jumped into the invisible queue, and walked out five minutes later. It took me an extra minute longer than everyone else because I teared up from the swab up my nose and then gagged when another was shoved down my throat. The kids anticipated it, so they waited to see it happen. They giggled.

We grabbed something to eat and expected results before going to sleep, or at the latest, the first alert on my phone when I woke up. Over the past year, we've done this so many times that it was as routine as flossing.

I ran through our pre-trip checklist while everyone was at school the following day. Because of all my mistakes, lessons learned, and heightened security, I checked it again.

As of 8:30 a.m., we didn't have any test results. Our flight wasn't until the afternoon and was still eight hours away. We had nothing to worry about. If we took our test at noon yesterday, we would get it in another four hours at the latest. It was a 24-hour test.

It was a short school day, and the kids arrived home just past noon. They put away their school stuff and did some final packing. Maricar was on her way, and I sent her a quick WhatsApp note.

"You get the results yet?"

"No. Did you?"

"No."

"Should we be worried?"

"We still have a few hours and can't do anything about it right now."

"Okay."

We ate a quick snack and as usual, it was a scramble out the door. It was 1 p.m., and we walked across the street to catch the bus. Maricar met us there, and I handed her bag over to her.

I'm starting to get nervous, and I refresh my email every five minutes. Nothing.

"Will we be able to use the lounge?" asked Jero.

"They are still closed because of the pandemic. We'll grab a snack when we switch buses. Is that okay?" answered Maricar.

"Currywurst and pommes?"

"Sure."

I sent an urgent email describing our situation, including all our information and a request for a quick response. I sent it twice, just in case.

The bus ride was 80 minutes with one transfer. I reassured myself that everything would be okay. It was probably because they were a little busy, and the results would come any time now. We got off the bus and waited ten minutes for our connection.

"Daddy, you said we can get a snack," said Jero.

"Right. Here's five euros. We have ten minutes before our bus comes so that means you have five minutes to get something at the store. Hurry up."

Jero, Lea, and Feris took off and left their bags with me.

How long had it been since I last checked? Still nothing. Everyone seemed so calm, but here I was worrying.

I experienced vivid flashbacks of Greece and getting denied boarding. I distracted myself by thinking happy thoughts of test results coming in one after the other. While the various scenarios are playing out in my head, the kids return with huge smiles and ice cream.

"I thought you said snack?"

"This is a snack!" Jero said as he handed me the change.

They continued chatting amongst themselves excitedly with the usual travel questions and banter.

"It's my turn to sit by the window," said Jero.

"Can we finish watching *Shrek* on the iPad?" asked Lea.

"Where are we staying?"

"How long is the flight?"

I turn to Maricar. "Should we be nervous?"

"Can you get in contact with them?"

"I can try calling, but I don't think it will work."

I called the number, and I went straight to hold.

It was 2:30 p.m. and only 90 minutes before our flight when we arrived at the airport. The first test result came in. Jero, negative.

This was a good sign.

As we snaked our way through security, Feris and my results came in. Negative.

Great, just two more to go. At this rate, we only had to worry about catching our flight.

I pull up my results again and then click a link that takes me to the fine print that says most results are available within 24 hours.

I'm standing in line, and I read it again.

"Most results?"

That's ridiculous. I started to talk out loud to myself.

"Well, what happens if results aren't ready before a flight? The only reason people take this test is to fly out. That's dumb."

Then I imagined the worst. *Oh no.*

What if Maricar and Lea were positive? What if that was why it took so long for the results to come back? Or, because they tested positive, they have to follow some reporting protocol that delays the whole process. It was only a matter of time before we got the virus, and it was happening to us now.

The lines were long, and we got through security with only 30 minutes to get to our gate and board our flight. We are still waiting for two tests. Anything can happen in 30 minutes.

At this point, I didn't know if I was more worried about getting a positive test or not receiving results in time. If it was the latter and the results were positive, then it would be good if we weren't on the plane because we would potentially infect other people and could get stuck in another country. Regardless of the outcome, I prepared myself to accept any fate.

This was Greece all over again. If we couldn't board because the results were late, we would find a way to move forward.

"Maricar, can you start looking up later flights?"

"There is a flight at six and another at eight. All with EasyJet, but there are limited seats."

We had our contingency plan in place.

If the results didn't come in the next 20 minutes, we would catch a flight two hours later when our results were sure to be in.

"Should we buy the 6 p.m. flight just in case, then?"

"Hold on. Refresh. Refresh. Refresh. Nothing."

No time to think. We walked straight into the boarding line and had our paperwork ready.

"Your boarding passes?"

I pull up digital copies saved into my Apple wallet.

"Identification?" I handed over the passports.

"Your COVID tests?"

I felt sweat on my back. "Yup." I pulled up each email individually, navigating between the results urgently.

"Can you show me Feris' test?"

"One sec. Let me pull it up. Here it is."

"Please go ahead."

I rushed everyone through, trying to avoid eye contact with the check-in attendant.

I looked over at Maricar and flashed her a big smile.

"What happened?"

"I don't know. I sort of blanked out."

"Did the other tests come in yet?"

"No."

"How did you get through?"

"I showed her the tests I had. In the process, she must have lost track of which ones she saw. Or maybe she had an internal clock and could only spend so much time with each passenger. She did a spot check, and luckily, it was one that I had."

It was like when we shopped at Costco. The person at the door can't spend time checking all 100 items in your cart so they just pick one or two and then move on.

"Will they check again once we get to Spain?"

"Probably, but we won't arrive for another two hours. The results will be in by then."

We all relaxed.

We arrived two hours later, and I first attempted to refresh my email. No service. I forgot we needed to buy data. I signed onto the Wi-Fi.

Why did it always take me forever to sign into free Wi-Fi? They made me click on a few ads, and I added my personal information, but when I opened a browser, it still didn't work.

Still nothing.

"Is your Wi-Fi working? I don't know if my email is refreshing."

Maricar confirmed that her Wi-Fi was working, and I refreshed my browser.

"No new emails. Not even spam. Just a survey from EasyJet asking about our recent flight."

"Why are you worrying? This is Spain, not Germany. At least, I don't think—"

Maricar didn't even finish her sentence. With the other hundreds of other tourists, we were funneled down a long corridor with various attendants holding up warnings to have your test results ready for inspection. Up ahead, I saw them stopping each group to review tests.

We weren't out of the woods yet.

"What are we going to do?" asked Maricar.

"We got this far, let's play it cool. I think we'll be okay since we aren't in Germany and rules can be bent."

Maricar and I didn't say anything to the kids. This was our burden, and I didn't want them to worry about what was potentially nothing.

I scanned the attendants and targeted the one taking the least amount of time with each tourist.

I channeled as much confidence as possible, acted like I was in a rush, and overwhelmed the person with English. For added effect, I had the kids crowd close while I rapidly flipped through my phone, showing our test results.

She waved us through. Once again, I rushed everyone through without looking back.

"How did you do that?" asked Maricar.

"Not sure. Someone is watching out for us." I responded.

We got to the hotel in our rental car, and as we checked in at around 7 p.m., Maricar's results came back negative—still nothing for Lea. We never got her results.

I began to contemplate alternative scenarios.

What if we were halted due to lack of test results and purchased tickets for a later flight? Our results still wouldn't have been ready on time, leading to two rejections at the gate, a wasted afternoon and evening at the airport, and two sets of unused tickets. Then, we would buy tickets for the next day's first flight, assuming the results would be in by then, only to be denied a third time. That would have been disastrous.

I'm grateful that things didn't unfold that way.

Instead, we enjoyed a brief getaway, relishing the resort, beaches, and hiking, and put all concerns behind us. We cherished this mini-vacation, aware that our European days were numbered.

In Their Words:
Mallorca

Jero (11):

- *Our place had a giant pool and open room. I brought my Lego Technic car, and I would take it apart and build something new every day, then test it on the beach. I even made it into a boat that would float using the tires.*

Lea (9):

- *You said it was going to be a bad hotel. Mommy said it was going to be a good hotel. On the way there, I looked at each hotel, wondering if this was the one. Happy when you said no to a bad one.*
- *The hotel was really nice. Clean. I remember liking it but can't remember anything about it or what we did there.*

Feris (6):

- *I remember a hike along the coast, and I crossed a rock bridge with Mommy.*

22

SATISFIED?

Switzerland, June 2021 (Week 98)

I asked Maricar, "What is the count now?”

“16 days of school. 24 days in Germany. 35 days until our Hong Kong quarantine.”

“Is it me, or does the past month feel like everything is moving fast?”

“I’m pretty sure the next few weeks will be even faster.”

If we weren’t at a Biergarten for extended goodbyes, we were squeezing in a last-weekend hurrah or checking off a Berlin bucket-list item.

“Do you see that group bringing a crate of bottled beer to the park?” I asked.

“Yeah. It happens a lot.”

“Let’s do that.”

“Do what? Carry a crate of beer to the park?”

“Exactly.”

"You know the beer will probably be warm, and we have to haul it to the park, right? And I don't even drink beer."

"That's all part of the fun. Berliner Kindl?"

"Natürlich!"

We secured a beer crate and invited our friends to Fischtalpark on a random Thursday. It was June so the weather and everyone's mood was fantastic.

It was funny how random activities snuck their way on the list. For example, there was nothing particularly special about bringing a crate of beer, but it provided an excuse to get a few families out for a picnic. Although we didn't have time to act on every idea, we considered them and were biased to action.

Spontaneity and a bias for action are qualities of some of the best friends one can have. Who are the people in your life who always come up with fresh adventures and are ready to act on them? When you have an idea, which friends are eager to join?

Maricar and I are like that for one another. It was how we often got ourselves into the unexpected because we had one another to say yes.

"What about Switzerland?" Maricar asked.

"What about it?" I said.

"We've got a four-day weekend coming up, and we can take an overnight train there. No testing required."

"That would be pretty cool to sleep on a train and arrive there in the morning."

"And maybe, we could stay at your boss's place," Maricar said.

You may be wondering, *when did he get a boss*? Between our adventures over the past two years, I picked up several consulting projects that kept me entertained while complementing our on-the-go lifestyle. One of those projects happened to be in Zurich.

"Did you know he lives on an estate? He's always talking about it, and he has hinted that he'd like to host us."

"Let's take him up on the offer. It would be rude not to."

We got an overnight train from Berlin to Basel. We thought overnight meant sleeper trains with beds in a compartment. When we got to our seats, we were trying to figure out how to convert the room for sleeping.

"Does a bed pull from the top?"

"Do these seats lay flat?"

After five minutes of fiddling with the chairs and not getting anywhere, we concluded they were just reclining chairs. There were six of them, three on each side facing one another. Because we reserved five of the six, there was a lone open seat that may either be reserved or used by someone at any time.

It would have been awkward if someone had taken the last remaining seat and been sandwiched between us all. We couldn't let that awkwardness happen. This trip was an eight-hour ride.

Every time someone passed, we made as much noise as possible and encouraged the kids to let loose.

"Kick their shoes off."

"Get comfortable."

So even if the seat was reserved, the person would take one look and keep walking. Every time someone passed, we silently celebrated.

We settled in once we got tired of watching the highlighter yellow rapeseed crops in the landscape. This was not the sleek overnight train from the movies I imagined and getting comfortable was not easy. I looked at Feris enviously, wishing I could find a position to help me fall asleep even if it was for just an hour.

The kids each found sleeping positions and passed out one after the other. Maricar was as bad as me. We just closed our eyes, hoping to sleep, but it never came. This was like my fruitless attempt to sleep at the Dublin airport food court booth.

When I got the initial invitation from my boss, whom I had known for five months but had never met in person, I wasn't sure if it was for dinner or an overnight stay. We showed up for dinner and, just in case, had a backup place booked to avoid an awkward situation.

"You and your wife will be staying in my room, and I have another for the kids. Will that be okay?" my boss offered.

"That sounds great, but where are you going to sleep?"

"Rather than using the rooms on another floor, I'll just sleep on the couch, so the maid doesn't have more work."

"You sure?"

"Absolutely. You are my guest."

And so, we stayed at a multimillion-dollar estate just outside Zürich with horses, its own river, a bowling alley, and a swan that would visit every morning.

It was priceless and was what the kids shared first if you asked them about the trip. It was a fantastic place, and if given the option, they would have stayed indefinitely instead of just the weekend.

We used it as a jumping point to explore Lucerne's old town, climb Mount Pilatus, ride a toboggan, and explore Switzerland's countless lakes.

We departed Europe on a high note, with one exhilarating experience after another. This final stretch was so remarkable that our kids would eagerly return to Germany without hesitation. It eclipsed many of the challenging moments from the past two years, reminding me that as parents, we don't need to be perfect. We just need to nail the beginning and end, and trust that everything in between will fall into place.

Before heading to Hong Kong, we squeezed in one last adventure in Turkey, a whirlwind trip scheduled immediately after the final day of school. We aimed to pack in as much excitement as possible before our impending three-week hotel quarantine.

In Their Words:
Switzerland

Jero (11):

- *We took a cable car up a mountain and then rode a summer toboggan. It's a giant metal slide you ride down and get pulled up by a cord. I think it was about a one-kilometer ride. There are people in front of you, and you control your own brakes, so we had to find the right speed. At first, I was really scared. We were in the Alps and had a great view while going down.*

Lea (9):

- *We had a car and went to pick up a bottle of wine because we were staying at your boss's estate. A mansion and then another mansion at the same place. We had a tour of the place to check out the river going through it, the bowling alley, and the horses. Afterward, we went for a swim before dinner.*

Feris (6):

- *Stayed in your boss's house. We had breakfast, and there were golden kiwis. I ate two, and Mommy told me to stop because I should be respectful.*

- *I remember the bowling alley and swimming in the river in front of his house. There were large gray fish with whiskers swimming upstream. There were also horses.*
- A *swan bit manang Lea's foot because she was messing with it. I remember riding a toboggan. We gave them a token, and they let us on. I rode with you, and Mommy rode with manang Lea.*

23
SQUEEZING IN IMPOSSIBLE

Turkey, July 2021 (Week 100)

School ended on Wednesday, June 30. We had to be in Hong Kong on July 11. This meant we had a tight ten-day window to do whatever.

What would even be possible? Where would we go? Where would we put our stuff?

Moving in itself is stressful, and here we were trying to figure out how to squeeze in a trip in the middle of an international move. Was this wild?

We knew that once we got to Hong Kong, we would go straight into quarantine for three weeks, and travel wouldn't be possible. It was a reality we had accepted over the past few months. So, even though we were tired, we knew we would have plenty of time to rest, and now was the time to get this out of our system.

The goal was to minimize costs and maximize our experience time. We bought two one-way tickets. The first was from Berlin to Istanbul, scheduled for Thursday, July 1, the day after the last day of school. The second set of tickets would bring us from Istanbul to Hong Kong ten days later.

This allowed us to move in the right direction and saved us the hassle of backtracking. From a symbolic standpoint, it was stupendous. We were leaving Europe and moving to Asia. In the middle of it all, we visited a city and country between the two continents with so much historical significance. It was too good of a fairytale to pass up.

For this fairytale to come true, what were the logistics?

In addition to ensuring that Germany was not on Turkey's pandemic restricted list, we also had to confirm that Turkey was not on Hong Kong's list. And, if Germany was a stickler for rules, Hong Kong was at another level, especially concerning the virus.

Our experiences traveling during a pandemic made us overly sensitive to rules, and we didn't want to get blindsided again, especially when the stakes were so high.

Relatively speaking, we didn't have much, but it was enough that we needed a solution, so we weren't lugging our eight 26-kilogram bags around a foreign country. If you kept score, we left Germany with less stuff than we brought. In this one way, our small basement apartment was a blessing because it forced us to keep a minimalist lifestyle.

We didn't have room to accumulate odds and ends, and we were discerning shoppers. It also helped that we were moving to a country where we wouldn't need our bulky winter gear. While others were paying for shipping and dealing with the headaches that come with stuff, we could enjoy a departure as if we were heading out on another holiday.

After making a few inquiries, I found a hotel in Istanbul and then negotiated terms so we could leave our bags while we traveled around the country. With the void in tourists over the past two years, they were more than happy to accommodate our request.

"We just leave our bags in the lobby?"

"Yes. Don't worry, there's always someone here."

I was skeptical. I hoped our bags were still there when we returned.

We divided our time between the cultural explosion and architectural wonders of Istanbul's mosques and bazaars, to Cappadocia's unique rock formations and Instagrammable hot air balloons.

When we were deciding on which coastal Turkish Mediterranean city to visit, it was either Antalya, the country's Capital of Tourism, or the resort town of Ölüdeniz known for its Blue Lagoon's turquoise calm waters. After Istanbul and hiking through Cappadocia, we chose the laid-back latter option.

Regardless of if we were at the hotel pool, the lagoon or at a restaurant, the sun would get eclipsed throughout the day by hundreds of paragliders that jumped from the nearby Babadag Mountain and descended on the beach. On our last day, we wanted to see what the hype was all about, so we took a bus to the top of the mountain and watched groups jump one after the other. The kids were a bit envious.

We returned back to town and while the kids were getting their daily late afternoon dose of ice cream, I wandered up to one of the many tourist vendors lining the street. It was not clear if they sold me or I talked myself into it, but I booked a paragliding trip set to leave in an hour.

"Everybody, finish your ice cream and get your shoes on. We are going up."

Here we were, going back up the winding road we had just come down.

As we were putting on our gear, I couldn't help but notice our guides huddling together. They were trying to time the jump before the wind picked up and come up with a strategy for Feris, who at five and maybe 40 lbs. when wet, was under the recommended height and weight threshold. This was news to me as it wasn't a problem when I made the booking.

Their solution was to have her go first, taking advantage of the mild winds and then have two guides hold her in place while the third, her pilot, jumped with her off the mountain. I found this solution amusing and was relieved that we wouldn't have to endure the embarrassing drive down the mountain, which was infamously dubbed the "drive of shame".

It was the final jump of the day, during the golden hour just before sunset. We had crystal-clear skies and breathtaking views of the lagoon, the endless sea, and the town below. After taking it all in, my pilot asked if I wanted to go faster and do some tricks. Why not? I gave him the universal thumbs up, and he immediately picked up speed, spiraling in circles. I grew nauseous, unable to tell which direction was up or down, but I figured I was only doing this once, so I continued to flash my thumbs up. I forced a smile as he directed me into awkward poses, reassuring me it would look great on the 360.

We touched down, and still dizzy, I walked in a crooked line. The kids, who had arrived earlier, were radiating energy and all smiles.

"What took you so long?" they asked.

When we returned to Istanbul to prepare for our flight, our bags were fine, which wasn't surprising after nearly two weeks in the country. Turkey had treated us to best-in-class hospitality, besides serving us some of our best meals.

In Their Words:
Turkey

Jero (11):

- *Prior to traveling to Turkey, I read* Refugee. *There is a scene where the main character's family hires a coyote to take them to the border, and they get taken advantage of. I thought it was going to happen to us, so I was scared every time we hopped in a car or bus.*
- *Cappadocia is in the middle of nowhere with lots of rock structures in a very dry area. We did a lot of hikes, including through the Love Valley. I remember learning why it's called the Love Valley and even got lost at one point. Luckily, we made it back before it got dark. The other highlight was riding a hot air balloon. We left really early in the morning. I thought we were going to get kidnapped because it was a big van, and we were driving into the fields in the dark. When we got to the site, we could watch them fill up 100s of hot air balloons with flame throwers. It was pretty cramped, but everyone had a section, and the views with the sunrise were really nice. There were lots of things to see, including a large pack of dogs that were running around and a different view of the rock structures that we hiked through the day before.*
- *There were things* [loudspeakers on tall minarets] *that would tell you it's time to pray. It was really loud, and someone would*

be singing. I think there was one at 6 a.m. or 9 a.m., and it would wake you up.

- *When visiting Turkey, we left most of our luggage in Istanbul at our hotel lobby while we traveled around the country. I was afraid that my Nintendo Switch and my Swiss Army knife would get stolen. It was the first thing I checked for when we got back. It was still there, and I was relieved.*

Lea (9):

- *Lots of nice people. Needed to go on public transportation and the old people would even give up their seats.*
- *My favorite restaurant had cats everywhere and had unique, bright furniture. I had baklava, a wafer cake. They served complimentary tea that was orange and tasted like Fanta. It was so good we went to the place twice.*
- *When we were in Cappadocia, the restaurant gave us three times what we ordered. Our server was so nice, and the food was inexpensive.*
- *Saw lots of temples or castles* [mosques] *that looked bright. We had to take off our shoes before going in.*
- *Got lots of ice cream. Turkish ice cream is all about how they serve it. There's a guy with a hat and a long spatula. He would make you look like a dum dum by tricking you with two cones and snatching it out of your hands so quickly.*
- *In Ölüdeniz, we went paragliding on a gigantic runway.*

- *I had to wear a backpack that was attached to my guide. He also had a GoPro stick and filmed it in 360. We glided left and right and landed in a park with other paragliders. I was one of the first to land and waited on the swing. Everyone complained about being dizzy because of the tricks. I was fine. I guess I didn't do those things.*

Feris (6):

- *We went hiking into a canyon, and I had to pee. When there was no one around, I crouched down and did my business. Toward the end of the hike, there was someone that hiked with us and helped us cross different hard sections. It then got really hard, and you had us stop.*
- *We were trying to take a picture next to a waterfall and Mommy was trying to avoid the water because she recently got a tattoo.*
- *I remember eating next to a river, and they had tables along the walkway. While eating, we put our feet into the water, which was really refreshing. Later, the water level rose, and we had to leave.*
- *Paragliding. They put me on a backpack sort of thing and held me by my arms and legs, and then they threw me off the cliff. It was so much fun. I was wearing my pink sandals. I could see Ölüdeniz, and the lagoon water all the way down.*

24

DOES EVERYONE KNOW SOMETHING WE DON'T?

Istanbul, July 2021 (Week 102)

It was midnight, and we were in the largest lounge ever at the Istanbul Airport. They had a pool table and all the baklava you could eat. Our flight wasn't until 1:50 a.m., so we enjoyed all the amenities.

"Are you sure you have everything?" I asked Maricar.

"Yeah," she responded.

"Did you review the email on protocol?"

"Yeah."

"How about that online form from this morning?"

"What form? I'll fill it out now."

"What else?"

"We have all our paperwork. I'm worried about the COVID tests."

"Why? We got them done at this airport, and they should be good. It was also completed well within the specified window."

"I know. The problem is that Hong Kong might not recognize the Turkish authority that administered the test."

"Really?"

We would find out soon enough.

Hong Kong was one of a handful of places, including Australia, Canada, Vietnam, China, New Zealand, and Singapore, with a zero COVID policy to address the global pandemic. The goals of zero COVID were the same, but each country implemented different restrictions to get it done.

What's the Zero-COVID Policy?

The Zero-COVID Policy is based on the belief that COVID was a highly contagious disease and that any case is one too many. Once it was loose in the population, it was assumed to spread rapidly and couldn't be contained. Hong Kong and China had a similar experience 20 years ago when SARS put everyone's life on pause, and a huge percentage of the expat population fled back to their respective home countries. It took years to recover, and the wounds were still fresh for some.

What did this look like in Hong Kong?

For a densely packed population of nearly eight million, there were fewer confirmed cases each month. And, more than likely, imported. To put this in perspective, the rest of the world's daily confirmed cases were over 100 per 100,000. Hong Kong was <1 per 1,000,000. And during the summer of 2021, when the world thought the global health crisis was in the rearview, the Delta variant, which was twice as contagious, was wreaking havoc on the rest of the world.

If we wanted to escape the virus, there was nowhere safer than Hong Kong. But the pursuit of zero COVID came at a cost.

Anyone entering the region was required to undergo a minimum two-week hotel quarantine. It was three weeks if you or someone in your party didn't have at least two COVID vaccinations. Upon arrival, they tested you. You couldn't leave the airport containment zone until your results were negative. Then, you were escorted in a shuttle with drivers wearing hazmat suits to your prebooked and prepaid hotel. After entering your room, you were not allowed out until your quarantine period was over.

The government required daily self-testing and temperature checks. People in hazmat suits would visit you every few days and administer PCR tests.

And even if someone was willing to go through all this, many countries were banned from entering if local cases crossed an acceptable threshold. Certain airlines were forbidden to fly to Hong Kong if they didn't meet strict COVID prevention protocols.

What happened if you tested positive? What happened if you broke quarantine?

Testing positive would extend your quarantine until you tested negative. There were instances of quarantine lasting months. If you broke quarantine—meaning if you stepped outside your door—the government would heavily fine and then penalize you with an additional week.

There were designated quarantine hotels, and all costs had to be paid in advance. These hotels were limited and often booked months ahead. They wouldn't even let you board the plane without a confirmed hotel reservation.

What did this mean for us?

We were diligent about keeping our paperwork in order. We had copies of all our vaccinations, work visas, and school acceptances, filled out and rechecked the prearrival paperwork, and even had our history of COVID testing.

We doubted whether the test we took in Istanbul would be accepted. Would the agency that conducted the test be recognized in Hong Kong?

Running through the zero COVID overview and entry requirements were a mouthful. It was hard to believe we decided to move here.

"This can't be right. Gate 17. Are we at the right gate?"

"That's what it says. Could the flight be canceled?" asked Maricar.

I refreshed my phone, and the gate was the same. It could be that the update hasn't been sent yet, so I looked at the departure board.

"Gate 17. We are at the right place. Maybe we are just too early."

We approached the gate and confirmed all the flight details. And because of the bundle of paperwork required to enter Hong Kong, the staff started proactively checking it 45 minutes before boarding.

For a 747 flight, we were surprised at how few people there were.

They began checking our paperwork.

"Passports?"

"Here."

"Hotel reservations?"

"Here."

"Visas?"

"Here."

"Tickets?"

"Here."

"COVID tests?"

"Here."

"Vaccinations?"

"Here."

All clear. That was easy.

We boarded the 747, and after a quick headcount, we determined there was more crew than passengers. There were at least two entire rows for each of us.

"Can I move seats?" Lea asked me.

"Sure. Get comfortable and try to get some sleep. It's a long flight."

"Do you think they will let me sit in business class?"

"The worst they can say is, no. Go for it."

Lea didn't ask.

Was the empty plane a red flag? Who in their right mind would voluntarily go to Hong Kong and subject themselves to a hotel quarantine? Will it be worth it?

On the way to Hong Kong, we had a layover in Thailand for an hour. We weren't allowed to leave the plane.

"Are we there yet? What's going on?" I asked.

"There wasn't a stopover on the itinerary, so I think we are just getting fuel," Maricar responded.

After 30 minutes, a new crew boarded.

Even the crew and pilots weren't exempt from COVID rules. I learned later that this was a process that airlines used to minimize quarantine for their crew. Every time someone re-entered the country, they were hit with an automatic quarantine. No exceptions.

We arrived at 8 p.m. at an empty airport. The sky-high ceilings and open space made sounds echo. Before the pandemic, this was the world's busiest for cargo and one of the busiest for passengers, connecting Asia to the rest of the world.

We were tired but hyperalert of the hospital-like conditions and staff escorting us everywhere. There were also signs everywhere scaring us with fines. I hadn't looked up the conversion yet, but 10,000 Hong Kong Dollars (HKD) was a fine I didn't want to get.

After taking in the scene and becoming overwhelmed, I gave the kids a quick pep talk.

"We are in another country, and they take rules seriously. Best behavior, got it?"

They nodded their heads.

We and the other zombie-like passengers were funneled through a dozen or so processing stations.

My mind raced as I took it all in and saw it as an experience. How many people could say they have first-hand experience of something like this? Based on the few people coming into the country, not many.

First stop? Paperwork check.

Second stop? We were issued a lanyard with our identification and given a sheet with all the steps before they released us. There were a dozen items on the list.

Third stop? Testing. I paired up with Feris, and we were escorted to a booth. Feris went first and then watched me as I was tested. As expected, I gagged and teared up when it was my turn. Would I ever get used to these tests?

One benefit is that there were no lines, and we were constantly on the move. After shuffling around from station to station for 30 minutes, things slowed down after our test.

We were given a sandwich, chips, water, and a choice of Oreos or Ritz cheese sandwiches.

I whispered to the kids, "Grab two. You don't know how long we could be waiting."

Then, we were each assigned a separate desk in a huge waiting area similar to conditions for the Scholastic Aptitude Test (SAT). From what I understood, we were supposed to wait here until our results came back. There was no notice of how long this would take. We sat there in complete silence.

I imagined that if this were in the US, you'd have kids running around, people playing loud music or talking loudly, and endless complaints. Instead, no one got out of their seats, and it was eerily silent except for the airport ventilation.

The Wi-Fi was good, and I hoped that the charge on my phone would last. The kids found ways to distract themselves by eating, sleeping, trading around the iPad, or fidgeting.

I wondered, *is this what they do in class when bored?*

After every half hour or so, they would call out numbers, and a batch would quietly leave together. What would happen if someone tested positive? Did they send in special forces to detain the individual?

Because people were seated based on when they took their test, we knew that we would be called soon.

"178, 179, 180, 181, 182, 183, 184, 185, 186."

They called our number.

"Grab your stuff, and let's go," I cheered.

Once we got our negative results, we were given documents to sign. It was our quarantine order and all the fine print of what we could and couldn't do. I read it twice, making sure that we didn't miss anything.

I assumed most people took the paperwork and just signed it. I could tell that the person was getting impatient with me.

By the time we were done, it was just past midnight, meaning we spent three hours going through processing. It wasn't as bad as I expected, and it was pretty efficient for the number of steps to complete to enter the country. But, going through this experience once, to say I went through it, was enough for me.

We found our duffel bags and boarded an assigned minibus. A person in a hazmat suit drove it, and he took us directly to our hotel.

No words were exchanged. I hoped they knew where they were going.

We were all tired, but I had everyone look out the window.

"Take it all in while you can. You aren't going to see the outside world for three weeks," I said.

This was a city. I had no idea where we were or where our hotel was located relative to the rest of Hong Kong. But the lights were bright for midnight, and the freeways were empty. Skyscrapers and what I believed to be housing shot into the sky, packed together like huge Lego structures.

We passed a port. This was the first time I had seen so many cranes and shipping containers in one place. I tried to get the kids excited, but they were beat. I got it—it had been a long 24 hours.

We arrived at our hotel, and I started sweating while walking the ten meters from the minibus to the hotel lobby. It was in the middle of the night, and it was so humid. Being indoors and avoiding this weather was going to be good.

Welcome to the Dorsett Wanchai!

As far as accommodations are concerned, we lucked out. Originally, we were issued two separate rooms, and because they were fully booked, they denied our request for connecting rooms. The plan was for Maricar and I to divide and conquer.

Lea is great on her own, but as a middle child, she gets territorial around her siblings and can throw a good tantrum. Maricar and Lea would be a team, and I would take Jero and Feris.

Another option we considered was Maricar getting her own room for two weeks while I babysat all the kids for three weeks. This would allow her to get out one week early to take care of housing and logistics ahead of schedule.

We playfully considered the scenario of Maricar and I sharing a room and letting the kids be on their own. Not only would we have gotten out early, but the two weeks without kids would be a honeymoon. We looked into it and discovered that at least one adult had to be in the room. Darn.

A week before our arrival, there was a Delta variant outbreak in the UK. Hong Kong moved quickly to ban all flights from the country, and because most expats were from there, rooms were freed up, allowing us to get adjoining rooms.

This now meant that we didn't have to separate. This was a good thing, right?

As an aside, anyone from the UK who wanted to get into Hong Kong at the time had to first travel to a non-restricted country for a week and then fly over. For those that were optimistic, they saw it as a forced holiday. The hoops that people had to jump through during the pandemic were excessive at times.

Although we were physically in Hong Kong, it was challenging to fully comprehend that this was our new home until we could truly experience it. Thus far, everything had unfolded smoothly, and all that remained was to navigate quarantine.

We were exhausted and eager to slow down. Following the hectic past few months, the kids were ready for a period of relaxation and a whole lot of nothing.

How difficult could this hotel quarantine possibly be?

In Their Words:
From Istanbul to Hong Kong

Jero (11):

- *When we first got to Hong Kong, we spent a long time in the cold airport. All the shops were closed, and it was empty. Even though we were there for over two hours, it all passed by really quickly.*
- *On the way to the hotel, there were so many lights from all the buildings.*

Lea (9):

- *We took a Turkish airline and flew at night. Quickly after we got on, they dimmed all the lights. There were so many vacant seats. I'd say there were four people for every 20 rows on a giant airplane. My dad asked if we could go to first class. They said no, but we could occupy any of the open seats. We had a lot of options.*
- *Because it was a long flight, they gave us pouches with handy things like a toothbrush and eye mask.*
- *After we landed, we had to go through a large hallway that was bright with escalators. We then had to get tested by people in full-body hazmat suits, which I thought was really weird. At*

one point, we got free Ritz crackers because we had to wait a while for our COVID test results.

Feris (6):

- *It was so fun. We brushed our teeth on the plane, which was weird. They gave us pillows and blankets and manang Lea and I had our own row.*
- *We couldn't watch TV because Mommy wanted us to sleep.*
- *When we first stepped out of the airport, we were behind a bus. I thought it was hot because of that, but when it moved, I realized it was just really hot and humid in Hong Kong. It was midnight.*
- *We took a minibus to our hotel. I was tired and had jet lag. When we arrived, it was really nice. I miss Dorsett Wanchai.*

25

LOCKED DOWN FOR 21 DAYS

Hong Kong, July 2021 (Week 103)

The door closed.

"Don't ever open the door unless someone knocks on the other end. Got it?" I told the kids.

"Why?"

"Well, if we do, then we can get fined a lot of money and might even have to stay here longer."

I like to think that everything in life is preparation.

If there were a pre-quarantine questionnaire that would assess suitability, it would look something like this:

Have you lived in a small space for an extended period? *Check.*

Have you shared that space with people 24/7? *Check.*

Do you know how to entertain yourself? *Check.*

We braced for the worst. However, if you asked the kids, this was one of their favorite experiences ever. I should have known that they would thrive. Every time we traveled, their favorite part was returning to our hotel or Airbnb. The more time out of the elements, sitting around, and doing nothing, the better.

I don't know if this is the result of our adventurous pace while exploring or if they are, by their nature, homebodies.

Our Hong Kong home for the next three weeks was the Dorsett Wanchai, your standard Western hotel on Hong Kong Island. We had two rooms at 300 square feet each. The queen and twin beds in each room were comfortable, but they took up most of the room, leaving us with limited space for anything else.

We were on the twenty-fifth floor, which, by Hong Kong standards, was not very high. We were too far from the ground for people-watching but low enough that other buildings towered over us.

What was there to see?

Traffic and, sometimes, sports cars, racing small stretches from one stop light to the next.

The rooftop cockatoos would appear at dusk every day as if on cue and then fly from one building rooftop to the next.

At night, a sliver of an opening between the buildings gave us a peek at the sea and the world-famous Victoria Harbour Light Show. It was the reflections on the water.

There was a tower with lights on the top, and at every hour, it changed to a different color. We tried to figure out the pattern.

The highlight was a giant building-sized Chanel poster from across our room with a woman advertising a bracelet. They replaced that poster during our quarantine, and we saw the whole process.

We spent much of our days looking out the window, at the world we would eventually explore.

The five of us, *and* all of our luggage from Berlin, had to fit in the two rooms. We tried to keep things contained and orderly, so it didn't feel like an episode of hoarders. Our eight humongous duffel bags were stacked in a corner, threatening to topple over.

"Daddy, where is my notebook?" asked Lea.

"Do we have any more paper?" asked Feris.

"Can you get my sweater? I'm freezing," asked Jero.

The bags weren't labeled, and I crossed my fingers, hoping the item in question was in the first one. The worst-case scenario was I would get to the bottom bag and have to restack everything. It was a good workout, and I was in no rush.

We weren't going anywhere and didn't have anyone to impress, so we got into a two-set clothing routine. While we wore one set, the other was drying by the window or on hangers that dangled from the extendable pull-up bar in the door frame between the two rooms.

As a COVID protocol, the windows were locked, and the AC always seemed to be too strong. We were often cold because we now lived a sedentary lifestyle and didn't control the airflow.

There was no room service or towel exchange. Keeping the place clean and clutter-free was an ongoing task we picked up from our time in Berlin.

The unsaid rule was that we each stuck to only one activity at a time. If we wanted to do something else, we would clean up our area before transitioning, while being mindful of what everyone else was doing.

When it was time to sleep, we slept. When we had to get energy out, we would work out. And so forth.

The highlight of every day was mealtimes. The hotel served breakfast, lunch, and dinner like clockwork and we built our schedule around the food. At the beginning of each week, we would put our orders on a checklist. There was the option for a Hong Kong or Western-style meal, or we could skip and get a small credit. These credits could then be used to order delivery items.

It was a puzzle. With 15 meals a day between the five of us, we tried to find the perfect combination to meet our nutritional needs without wasting food.

Because we were frugal and didn't want to introduce additional calories, we stuck with the available meals and ordered delivery only when desperate.

Which meals hadn't we tried yet?

How many meals do we order so we don't waste anything?

When should we use our credits for a treat?

Unlike in the real world, where snacking between and after meals was the norm, we were on a set meal plan. Every meal mattered. If we missed one or didn't feel like eating, we would have to wait for the next meal in a few hours.

The one meal we never found a taste for was congee, a rice porridge with a variety of toppings like ginger and mushrooms. It was a Hong Kong breakfast staple, but its flavor profile did not match our Western taste preferences. The first time it came, we refused to eat it, and then all we could think about was our next meal as our stomachs grumbled. We eventually put it on our do not order list.

After the first week, we celebrated by ordering delivery from one of the nearby restaurants. It was a Western-style pita that tasted incredible. We paired this with one of the assorted sodas in the fridge that we rationed out. We treated them as our emergency reserve in case we needed sugar.

I thought there was no such thing as a bad soda. After all, it was just carbonated sugar, stuff the body craves. Have you ever tried Schweppes Cream Soda? The kids took one sip and refused to drink anymore. The other three cans went untouched.

We liked having food around and being able to snack all the time. It brought us comfort, and with our once-active lifestyles, we were used to it. Recognizing that we would be lounging around, we refused to introduce snacks and stuck to the assigned meals. We only had a few moments of weakness.

"Have you heard of HKTV yet?" asked Maricar.

"We can order groceries, and have it delivered to our room as long as we order a minimum."

"Same-day delivery and prices are reasonable."

Part of what made this lockdown rewarding was seeing the restrictions as a benefit. If we switched our brains to think of this as something that we chose, then we could reframe everything as a way to help us. The meals were our introduction to Hong Kong cuisine, and the elimination of snacks was a forced fast to reduce our sugar intake and processed foods.

It worked most of the time.

"I'm going to place an order," I said. "What do you want?"

"Better question is, what don't I want? We should only get 'emergency' items."

"What does that mean?"

"Cereal, milk, cookies, chips, ramen, ice cream, and wine."

"In other words, comfort foods. Our stuff will be here later today."

I remember being hungry all the time. It was a combination of the extra time spent thinking about food and the finite portions they provided. I turned into Pavlov's dog. When mealtime approached, I would salivate just a little with the sound of a knock. Because we had two rooms and two doors, it would be an initial knock immediately followed by a second.

"Food is here!"

Everyone would start cleaning up their stuff.

"Can I open the door?"

They've been trained well.

"Sure."

Hotel staff would place the food outside our door on a chair. There would be five packaged meals that we struggled to finish, often leaving us in a food coma. Rather than having too much food, we started ordering and splitting up just four, leaving us a little hungry instead of a little too full.

Sometimes, we'd hear a ghost knock if it were past the usual delivery time.

"Did you hear that?" I asked.

Maricar responded, "I don't know."

"Check the door."

We would open the door and see an empty hallway. I would then phone in to see what the holdup was.

Between lunch and dinner was the longest stretch, and I became dependent on Lipton Tea to get through it. I've never been one to drink the stuff, but with the AC constantly pushing cold air into the room and the reduced calorie intake, I needed it to take the edge off. I became addicted to the yellow tea bags and even desperately made a special request to the front desk for more when we ran out. Toward the end of our stay, I looked at my teeth and couldn't believe how stained they had become.

To stay active, we had a daily morning workout that consisted of bodyweight exercises. I was used to going into autopilot when running, so the High Intensity Interval Training (HIIT) approach burned me out. It consisted of jump rope, pullups, burpees, and squats. It was challenging and required my complete focus, particularly for the jump rope and burpees. I was also barefoot, meaning every time I messed up jumping rope, I'd be punished with a whack on my feet. Burpees were always terrible. Every rep required a mental and physical push to get going. There wasn't an option to coast.

These were close quarters and other than the bathroom, there was no personal space. Someone was always around. If I didn't wake up early enough, the kids would watch me and start talking to me while I worked out. I gave them a quick look that meant, don't bother me. I felt sorry for the room below us, having to hear the jump rope slapping each morning. I'm sure they understood that we were all in the same boat, just trying to get through our time.

To mix things up, we had a few Tae Bo sessions. The kids were familiar with Billy Blanks from our earlier Iceland and Italy quarantines. Sometimes, we let them off the hook with an easy "Yoga with Adriene" session or turned things up with the German "Growing Annanas" HIIT workouts.

To exercise our minds, we spent the mornings on the major subjects of math, reading, and writing. From what we heard about the Hong Kong international curriculum, we had work to make up for the COVID gap years.

When everyone finished their work, afternoons and evenings were for screen time. The kids got a lot of it.

For live TV events, there was the Summer Olympics in Tokyo, where we benefited from being in the same time zone. Even without skateboarding experience or understanding of how points were awarded, the X Games became our favorite. The athletes were the definition of cool.

There was *Nintendo's Zelda: Breath of the Wild* in the afternoons. For two years, Jero had been begging to play this action-adventure game, possibly, the greatest ever created. We finally caved, knowing that quarantine would be the ideal setting. Jero played while Feris watched. Quarantine was a hit because they became infatuated with the game.

Jero's greatest moment of triumph came when he defeated Thunderblight Ganon, arguably the hardest boss in the game. After failing countless times over three days and starting to think it was impossible, he overcame the electricity axe, dashing attacks, and paralyzing moves to defeat him. He jumped up with his hands raised and flashed a smile that stretched from cheek to cheek. He was this close to saying, "I am invincible," just like Boris from *Goldeneye*.

Lea spent her afternoons disappearing quietly into YouTube, watching Brent Rivera and sssniperwolf amongst other internet personalities. She would binge-watch reaction videos and vlogs and then return with tales of random content she covered.

She was a preteen, spending quite a bit of time in front of the screen. And that was okay because if there was ever a time to do it, now was it.

There was always a movie to look forward to at night, and we used the opportunity to get all the classics under our belt, like *Dirty Dancing*, *Shawshank Redemption*, and *Cast Away*. Bedtime would never go past 10 p.m. If it did, nights and days would soon start blending into one another, and the whole schedule would crumble.

Given how quickly the kids settled into the structured routine, this was easy. Getting ready for the day, working out the body and mind, and then the playtime wasn't far from what we did for months at the beginning of the pandemic or when we were in quarantine. It was a forced routine that kept us productive and sane.

I asked, "Did you hear a knock?"

"I think so, but it's too early for lunch, and there was no scheduled COVID test. It could be a random kid playing a prank and knocking on all the doors," Maricar responded.

"Should I answer it then?"

"Yeah. What do we have to lose?"

At the door were three small boxes.

"Open it up."

Inside each box was a different puzzle.

It wasn't much, but it was a nice surprise from the mundane and a way to entertain the kids for an hour.

It was 2 p.m.

"Another knock?" I asked

"Go check," Maricar said.

"Pineapple buns and milk tea. Score!" Jero said, peeking out the door.

Fridays became our favorite. Each morning, there was a little present for the kids. However, the afternoon was the real highlight with a popular Hong Kong dessert always paired with milk tea. This is where we got our first authentic egg tarts and mango pudding. They even included a card that shared a bit of history on each item. A taste of the outside . . . we couldn't wait for the real thing.

These small surprises lifted our spirits and gave us something to look forward to.

What did we learn?

The Serenity Prayer was something I learned from twelve years of parochial school growing up, and repeated it countless times, but it really sank in during these three weeks.

God, grant me the serenity to accept the things I cannot change, the courage to change the things I can, and the wisdom to know the difference.

We had decided to move to Hong Kong, meaning we chose to quarantine for three weeks. There was no way around it, and we embraced the slower lifestyle with open arms. We loosely structured our days so there was just enough variety so we didn't grow restless.

Most importantly, instead of seeing this mandatory quarantine as three wasted weeks, we chose to reframe our mindset. For every instance we could frame our situation through a glass half empty or full perspective.

I missed running OR this was an opportunity to rest my body and develop other muscle groups.

We were cut off from social contact OR this was for personal time.

We were being sloths OR it was a restful change of pace from our active lifestyle.

We missed our favorite foods and snacks OR it was a cleansing fast and opportunity to try new foods.

We were trapped with one another OR we got to spend this time together.

We were wasting time OR we were having a once-in-a-lifetime experience.

Some people paid thousands of dollars for a weekend or week wellness retreat for this kind of life simplicity. We were getting it for three weeks.

Not everything was a *kumbaya* moment. There were the occasional moments of frustration with one another. The culprit was either someone having too much energy or being bored. Going for a walk was not an option. To solve this, we would make space for planks or jumping jacks to burn off energy, and there were always more math problems, a new book, or a writing prompt ready to go if someone needed a healthy distraction.

If we ever felt trapped, we'd channel the serenity prayer reminding ourselves to use this time to do the things we wouldn't have done.

We had already experienced quarantine, so this wasn't entirely new to us. The past two years of living together, primarily through a global pandemic, had prepared us for everything that hotel quarantine could throw our way.

The kids will always look back on quarantine with fond memories. There was no hiking or aimless wandering. In fact, we encouraged them to sleep in for the first time ever. They enjoyed nearly unlimited screen time and even each had their own bed - what more could a kid want?

When it was time to leave, I might have heard the kids express a hint of reluctance.

In Their Words:
Dorsett Wanchai Quarantine

Jero (11):

- *The food was really good. The best was the pineapple bun and milk tea every Friday. It just might have been my favorite part of the week.*
- *My main motivation during this time was to play* Legend of Zelda's Breath of the Wild *on the Nintendo Switch. To do that, I had to first exercise, read, and do my work. If I finished everything, I would play from 2 to 6 p.m. It was fun because it was new, and I got really good.*
- *We were pretty high and could see quite a bit. I'd watch the cockatoos and all the fancy cars pass by. I got the impression that Hong Kong was rich because of that.*

Lea (9):

- *We got sent to our hotel, Dorsett Wanchai. It was two rooms that were joined together. There was a meal plan, and we put in our orders a week in advance.*
- *I thought we would be chilling and watching TV for three weeks. Actually, we had to do a lot of exercise and work before we could even see a screen.*
- *They had robes with white belts. We would use those as whips. There was a big bed that we would jump on because we would*

get bored.

- *We got purple flowers from the hotel as a gift and had to take care of them during the three weeks. I was amazed because I ripped off a bud, and the flower kept blooming, so I thought it would stay alive forever. When it was time to go, we left the plants in the room.*

Feris (6):

- *I liked staying at the hotel.*
- *One dish I liked had vegetables, rice, and meat. I think it was duck. I hated congee. Flavorless soup with soggy rice and little veggies inside. It was cold. It would have been better if it was like the one in Boracay with fried garlic.*
- *I was always thirsty. We had a box of water bottles with a blue cap and wrapper. Whenever we ran out, we would call to get more and then they would drop off a new box.*
- *They gave us presents and treats. Painting things and teddy bears—that made me happy.*
- *We had to do a spit test, and I cried. There was a bottle, and you had to spit a certain amount. You were rushing me because there were people waiting outside for the sample.*
- *We played* Legend of Zelda Breath of the Wild. *Actually, I just watched while Jero played.*
- *There were two beds in one room. One bed in the other room. Lea and I shared a bed, and we were always fighting and getting consequences like kneeling. It was tiring.*

- *I actually liked our quarantine hotel because it was nice and clean. It was much better than our apartment in Berlin. From our window, we had a view of construction.*
- *I was unhappy about leaving because I was going to miss it.*

26

OFFICIALLY DAY ONE

Hong Kong, August 2021 (Week 105)

It was a Sunday.

I called the front desk last night.

"Our quarantine orders state that our last day of quarantine is today. Does that mean I can go for a run tomorrow morning?"

"Not really. You can leave as early as midnight, but once you leave, you can't come back in."

"That's good to know. And for tomorrow, do we then just leave whenever we want?"

"Not exactly. Please call the front desk to let us know when you are ready to leave. We will then send someone to grab your bags. Once the hallways and elevators are clear, we will call you down."

Stepping out the door was surreal because we had never made it this far or considered crossing the line for fear of getting slapped with a fine.

It was like Morgan Freeman in *Shawshank Redemption* when he was first released and asked permission before doing anything.

"Bathroom break, boss?"

"You don't need to ask me every time you need to go take a piss. Just go. Understand?"

We dropped off our paperwork, and when I was expecting a smile and congratulations, I received a stamp. This might have been a massive milestone for us after spending three weeks in quarantine, but for the hotel, this was another transaction they processed several times a day.

It was August, and as we stepped outside the hotel, we tasted the Hong Kong summer humidity. Three weeks in a temperature-controlled room didn't help us with this abrupt transition.

We were looking forward to so much, including seeing a different angle of our Chanel poster, learning what was around the corner, riding the tram, and seeing real people. Other than the people coming in as Darth Vader every week for testing, we hadn't had any contact with human beings.

As part of the moving package, the school covered the cost of quarantine and then one week at a hotel. Our new temporary home was the Harbour Plaza North Point, where we got a suite with a kitchen, a small dining area, and a decent view of the sea. Quarantine here would have been heaven.

We had three weeks to get situated before school started, and our priority was finding an apartment. At one point, when we were in quarantine, with too much time on our hands, we were considering renting an apartment sight unseen to make sure it would be ready in time. We didn't, so here we were on a mission to check that box off immediately.

We dropped off our stuff at the hotel, and the first action item was securing Octopus cards at the nearest Mass Transit Railway (MTR) station at Quarry Bay. These cards were conveniently used for everything. We loaded them up and quickly learned to treat them as our lifeline for getting around on buses, trains, and ferries and staying hydrated with drinks from 7-11 or any other store.

"Maricar, lead the way."

"First stop: the MTR Station. Second stop: Discovery Bay."

With Octopus cards in hand, we went to the bus stop.

"Look for the 6X."

"There it is."

"Check it out. On the floor they have lanes for lining up. That's new. I can imagine how long these queues can get during rush hour, especially since there are several buses that stop here."

"Do we all have our cards? Just tap it like everyone else."

"Hey look, it's the Dorsett Wanchai."

We were just there a few hours ago, and the kids were already getting nostalgic. Fresh quarantine memories came flooding back.

It was a simple bus ride, but we were taking it all in and trying to process it.

What language did people speak?

How did they dress?

How did people conduct themselves on the bus?

What did people carry with them?

"This is our stop."

"What now?"

"We need to find Pier 3 for Discovery Bay."

"Once we get there, our agent will meet us at the coffee shop and take us around."

The ferry ride was comfortable and only cost us $5 for adults and half that price for kids. It was as if all transportation was heavily subsidized and conveniently accessible with our Octopus card. The ride was a smooth 30 minutes, taking us from Hong Kong to Lantau Island. Besides the Kowloon and Hong Kong Island skyline views, we also saw Disneyland as we were coming into our port. With the happiest place on earth so close, we made a note to visit soon.

We got off the ferry and sized up Discovery Bay. I remember thinking, *the hype is real. It is a resort.*

Right off the ferry was a beach and an indoor mall with an ice skating rink. Everyone walking in or out was dressed like they were on a tropical vacation.

I had to say it.

"We weren't in Zehlendorf anymore."

We were on a mission and visited nearly 20 apartments that afternoon, determined to find our new home. We would have been taken around on a golf cart, but it couldn't hold us all so we settled for a private van. Not as cool, but it got the job done.

Before our tour, our real estate agent warned us multiple times that Hong Kong apartments were not like in America and that we should reset our expectations. Little did she know that for us, anything would be an upgrade. Our experience with humble accommodations was going to pay off.

We aimed to find a newer apartment with an open floor plan conveniently located near the school. We had a conservative budget, knowing that we would be on the hook for the tuition of one kid. The fees were comparable to the price of an American university.

I'm glad we opted to see these apartments in person. A walkthrough allowed us to visualize our setup and routines, understand our surroundings and get a feel for the commute to school. Most buildings were on a steep slope, and everything seemed twice as far with the humidity. These factors made it hard to judge walkability just from a map.

"Are we done yet?" asked Lea.

"I'm really hungry," chimed Feris.

"Me too. Here, eat this raisin bread. It will hold you over," I said.

"How many places are left?"

"Four, and based on the pictures, there is one I'm looking forward to seeing."

We didn't see the last two apartments. Our atrophied legs and AC-dependent bodies couldn't handle all this humidity and action on the first day. We saw enough. At least two to three flats would work to meet our needs.

"Give us an hour, and let's meet up again. The kids are hungry, and we will stack rank the 18 apartments."

We then parted with our agent, took our lists with scribbles, and got pizza to discuss things.

"Which apartment did you all like?" I asked the kids.

"The one with a pool," Lea shared.

"Remember that it only had two rooms. This would mean the three of you would share."

"We know."

"Are you sure? If we get that, I don't want to hear any complaints about space."

"We promise not to complain. So can we get it?" asked Jero.

"Mommy and I have to talk it over."

This conversation was like every instance where a child asked their parents for a dog, all while making hopeful but empty promises.

Yes. If we get a dog, I promise to love, walk, feed, and clean up after it every day.

The apartment the kids wanted was just over 700 square feet, modern with amenities, and close to the school. I liked it because the smaller space meant less to furnish, less to buy and ensured we stuck to our minimalist living roots. It eliminated the things that would isolate us from one another and distract us from the simple pleasures of life that mattered.

Maricar wanted at least a three-bedroom for each person to have more personal space. The squabbles over space and the headaches of figuring out where to put stuff still haunted her.

We decided to go with the kids' pick. It had two bedrooms, one bathroom and two small balconies. There was a nice lobby and pool, and it was one of the newer buildings in the area. The school, grocery store, and bus stop were all accessibly close.

As we settled in, it felt like a version of my favorite movie. Familiar, but different. The plot was the same, but the characters and setting were new. Every time we visited a new place or country, we quickly aimed to get our bearings and find our routine.

Fresh surroundings provided a new normal. It was an opportunity to discover new places and change stale habits.

Where would we go on our morning runs, and what would be the scene?

Where and how are we going to get groceries?

How would the weather affect us?

What's the daily commute to school?

Where can we go to get some air?

How does transportation work, and how far can it take us?

If we send someone for a walk, where will they go?

What stories would we share when describing our new neighborhood?

Securing an apartment and moving in was a swift process, thanks to Hong Kong's efficiency. From obtaining our Hong Kong identification cards to setting up utilities in the apartment, everything was streamlined.

With one major hurdle overcome, we had 100 more to tackle. Just as in Berlin, settling in brought us closer together as we explored our new city.

The honeymoon phase wouldn't last indefinitely, and I wondered when our first significant challenge would arise. It was only a matter of time.

In Their Words:
First Impressions of Hong Kong

Jero (11):

- *It was basically a cleaner Germany. Not as much trash, buildings were cleaner and newer. And because it rained so much, everything was really green.*
- *I thought that Hong Kong was a fancy place, that everything would be super expensive, and people were rich.*

Lea (9):

- *Stepped outside, our first time in civilization in nearly a month. I thought it was just going to be sunny, but not hot. Have you ever stood behind a bus? That's what it felt like.*
- *We took a black taxi. My dad asked if he was driving. He got into the front seat on the wrong side. In America, the front passenger seat is on the other side.*
- *We stayed in another hotel before moving into our apartment. The Harbour Plaza Hotel was big, and the food was nice. There was a pool, but I was disappointed. I thought it would be luxurious. It was warm, and I think it was because there were lots of kids in it.*

Feris (6):

- *I remember that it was hot and humid. That's all.*
- *When leaving our room for the first time, the elevators were so hard to find. I think they did this, so people wouldn't escape. Also, there were no buttons for floors in the elevator.*

27
REMEMBER, YOU SIGNED UP FOR THIS

Hong Kong, March 2022 (Week 137)

It was well before 6 a.m. and warm outside, but who am I kidding? At this point of the year, it was warm all the time. It was a nasty combination of hot and humid weather that made you sweat so much that you looked like you stepped out of a shower. Your shoes would squelch because they pooled up with sweat. It was gross, but you dealt with it.

Shoes, keys—I know I'm missing something—my mask. That's new.

I still couldn't believe I had to wear a mask while running. It was going to be like sucking air through a coffee straw. I felt like I would suffocate.

I put on my mask and started running. My body switched to autopilot, and then it was me and my thoughts.

Seven months have passed since our hotel quarantine. Now, we were in the midst of the fifth wave, and the world pandemic thanks to the Omicron variant that arrived last December. We first had a handful of imported cases a week that doubled and tripled in

January. In February, infections exploded from 1,116 cases to over 300,000 by the end of the month.

In response, schools had gone fully remote, and digital sign-ins were required everywhere. Most people had gone into isolation—some of them by force at Penny's Bay, a quarantine center right next to Disneyland.

Hong Kong turned heads globally when it "culled" thousands of hamsters supposedly carrying the virus and caused an outbreak in January. Circumstances were getting comically ridiculous. Each week, a neighbor or ex-pat would tap out and leave Hong Kong.

Our three-year milestone of living abroad was right around the corner. Everything since our first day had been a roller coaster. Maricar and I always wanted to take our kids on an adventure—we never pictured it playing out like this.

Initially, I had a definition of adventure as an unusual, exciting, or daring experience. I envisioned backpacking over mountains or exploring remote areas photographed in *National Geographic*. Over time, through our experiences and pandemic travel constraints, my definition and scope of adventure expanded. It became an approach for seeing the world — appreciating routine's beautiful consistency, embracing experiences with uncertain outcomes, and challenging myself to find adventure anywhere, even in our backyard.

Through the journey of all our extreme and local adventures, we've grown.

Courtney Dauwalter, the top women's ultrarunner and winner of three iconic 100-mile races (e.g., the Western States 100,

Hardrock 100, and the UTMB), is known for her athletic endurance and mental toughness. The latter becomes increasingly important the harder and longer the race goes.

After a full day of pushing your body and then summiting a mountain through the night by yourself, your mind flips a switch to protect the body.

"Stop running!"

In such moments, you need a mental strategy to convince your body to keep going. Courtney visualizes a file cabinet of experiences and problems she has encountered and ways she has tried to solve them. Then, when a problem comes up, she goes through that file cabinet, looking for possible solutions. She has quite the library with all the races and consistent wins under her belt.

We were in the thick of the pandemic, Hong Kong edition, pulling from our mental file cabinet of the past three years. We've been here before, accommodating remote learning, teaching within a limited space, and scratching our adventure itch when the world shut down.

We started by redefining our path. We believed there was another way to raise a family. It was a way to spend our best years being present and building strong connections while having an adventure together—a reimagined life.

We tested our hypothesis with an unscripted journey, operating with a self-imposed urgency and taking calculated risks. When blindsided by travel restrictions, we were resourceful, walked the fine line between stupid and adventurous, and completed our endurance quarantine.

Was surviving Iceland or each other in one bedroom for nearly two years more extraordinary? It's a toss-up.

Despite the headlines that get attention, my favorite moments are when we break bread at the dinner table. In another life, dinner was a chore to check off. We ate in shifts because our schedules were a matrix that didn't fit together. The focus was on getting food down, barking orders, and hurrying up so we could fit in one more busy task before bed.

Dinner today was at six or as soon as I finished cooking. Whatever has happened in the day or wherever we are, we come together to eat. We may have been sitting on makeshift chairs or squeezing around a table made for two, but we were together, talking and having honest conversations.

When this first became a ritual, we'd go around with everyone sharing a high and low or answering the question of the day: "What was something that made you laugh?" Now, there is never silence, and the kids use most of the airtime. Feris describes her recess game of playing house and how she played the daughter role with her friends. Lea shares her latest cheesy and sometimes borderline inappropriate pickup lines: "Excuse me, do you have a Band-Aid? I just scraped my knee falling for you." Jero oversells his physical performance at PE, reenacting how he dodged the balls.

The simplicity of our lives has eliminated distractions. We are present, and our surroundings help.

If I were to write a third part of this adventure, it would be "The Journey Goes On." Trapped in Hong Kong, we've created our own microadventures and have taken on the audacious family goal of conquering all four Hong Kong long trails—a total of 298 kilometers and 14,500 meters of elevation gain. We weren't going anywhere, and we informally decided that we were staying here indefinitely.

As we've had to do many times over the past few years, we sometimes needed to *decide* before we knew the *how* or the *what*. We had so many unknowns, but that's what makes life, life. Pursuing the unknown was how we got to where we are today.

At the time, I couldn't have known that in two months, Hong Kong would cut the hotel quarantine period in half, and that week, we would buy tickets to return to California for the summer.

I couldn't have known that in six months, they would remove all mandatory hotel quarantine requirements, and we would book tickets to the Philippines to visit Maricar's parents in Miagao, enjoy Boracay, and provide the kids with an authentic Pilipino experience.

I couldn't have known that in 12 months, we'd be in Thailand to indulge in the food and get pampered with massages, island hop in Palawan, and explore Hanoi, walking the same streets where I recovered from food poisoning.

I couldn't have known that in 18 months, we'd visit Japan during Sakura season, drive the Australian eastern coast from Sydney to Cairns in a neon green and purple Jucy van, survive two near-death experiences in the form of a hotel fire and a seven-car pile-up explosion, and hop from one Singapore hawker center to another.

I couldn't have known that in 24 months, Maricar and I would run the Macau marathon, take the train from South Korea's Seoul to Busan, travel around Taiwan in ten days, and celebrate the holidays in Bali, eating *ayam goreng* with our hands every other day.

And I couldn't have known that in 30 months, we would decide to move to Zurich to start a new chapter, only to pivot at the eleventh hour, listen to our gut, and return home to California to plant roots.

I couldn't have known these things.

In his book *Tuesdays with Morrie,* author Mitch Albom met weekly with his former professor, Morrie Schwartz, who is dying of ALS. They discuss all facets of life. Maricar gifted me the book when we were teaching in NYC a lifetime ago, and the following quote has stuck with me:

"Everybody knows they're going to die, but nobody believes it. If we did, we would do things differently," Morrie said.

"So we kid ourselves about death," I said.

"Yes. But there's a better approach. To know you're going to die, and to be prepared for it at any time. That's better. That way you can actually be more involved in your life while you're living."

Looking at the big picture and considering it a long-term journey, I'm uncertain about what lies ahead. I must remind myself that we deliberately chose this path, and we need to hang on loosely, for an unforeseen misadventure is inevitable.

While nearing the end of my run, I realize that I haven't felt this invigorated in a while. I contemplate extending it by adding an extra

5k, but then think better of it, assuming a household squabble over who finished the milk is likely unfolding.

Regardless, I'll be back out here tomorrow, steadfast and prepared, come what may.

In Their Words:
COVID in Hong Kong

Jero (12):

- *I remember having to wear a mask all the time. The only time we wore a mask in Berlin was when we were indoors. In Turkey, masks weren't a thing. Here, everyone followed the rules, so it would be rare to see someone without a mask.*

Lea (10):

- *I had a teacher who would call students out if they didn't wear their masks correctly. She would insult them with names like a sniffer. Everyone looked weird once they got rid of their masks. I imagined the bottom of their faces looking a lot different.*
- *Every month, the school would give each student six boxes filled with tests. We were supposed to take tests every day before school, but people were too lazy and would keep them in their lockers. With all the extra tests, I experimented to see if I could find COVID in the school. I swabbed the dirtiest places, and it would always come out negative. I wondered why we even needed to test.*
- *There were signs all over the place saying that you had to wear a mask. I still see them around. Reminders of the recent past.*

Feris (7):

- *I didn't really like the screen dividers between our desks. They were clear with black frames to hold them in place. We'd use them to insert our names. If you wanted to talk to the person next to you, you'd have to move your head to their side of the screen.*
- *Jasmine was my first friend, and Elise was my second. I went to Jasmine's house, which was on the other end of where the #9 bus went. But then, things got really bad in Hong Kong, and she moved away. I think it was to Copenhagen.*
- *It was hard to hear people when they wore masks. Teachers would pull down their masks when they were speaking. One teacher would spit when he talked, and it would get on me. He should wear a mask all the time.*
- *Good things happen on Wednesdays. It's a lucky day. We stopped wearing masks on a Wednesday. We got rid of the dividers also on a Wednesday.*

EPILOGUE

San Francisco, July 2022

One year after arriving in Hong Kong, we were at the airport again. But this time, with tickets for California to spend the summer with our friends and family.

We had come full circle.

It felt like we were gone forever and had changed so much, but things were as we had left it three years ago when we returned. Some people shared familiar ideas, routines, and stories.

"I got a promotion."

"I'm so busy, but we should hang out."

"I bought a new car. It's a huge upgrade from the previous model. Check it out."

"Jimboy is now doing x, y, and z. It will look so good on his college application."

They were still on the path and ahead on the game board. We were now playing another game.

And then there were others where the pandemic forced them to pause, reflect on their priorities, and question where their time was going. They started living in the now and were deliberate with their life choices. Some were minor, like negotiating their commute, and others were more momentous, like a career change, a physical move, or starting a family.

We were committed to staying in Hong Kong for at least one more year. Coming back reaffirmed our decision. We realized we weren't ready to be home permanently or plug back in. Like on the Monopoly board, we were only visiting.

There were two significant changes:

I had new nieces and nephews born during the pandemic.

The gas prices. I didn't think I'd ever see the day that gas was $6 a gallon.

People simultaneously admired us for what we were doing and confessed they could never do that. At one point, we thought the same.

We did all the things we could in California. We drove the Pacific Coast Highway, camped in Lake Tahoe, watched a San Francisco Giants game, attended a sold-out Las Vegas concert, and spent time in Hawaii. We alternated between In-N-Out and Mexican food every other day. I miss this food. We even got to celebrate my mom's 65th birthday.

I brought back to Hong Kong a dozen bottles of my favorite habanero hot sauce from Trader Joe's, and we were gifted ten family-sized boxes of Honey Bunches of Oats that took up a whole duffel bag.

The kids delighted in the attention and affection showered upon them by our friends and family, who spoiled them rotten. It was heartwarming to see, as I hope these fond memories will inspire them to want to return — someday.

Q&A WITH JERO, LEA, AND FERIS

December 2023

The kids have the final word. What do they think about all this?

- What is your favorite place, and why? Was there any place you did not enjoy? Why?
- Where is home for you? What do you miss about it? Do you get homesick? If yes, for what place?
- If you could live anywhere in the world, where would it be?
- What has been your favorite experience? Worst?
- What are the differences between your life abroad and life in California? How would you describe your lifestyle?
- What do you think about your parents' choice to leave the US and live abroad with you? If you had a choice, would you do it again? Why or why not?
- What do you think about the past five years?
- What advice can you give to a kid your age who is about to go live abroad for the first time?

JERO BAYANI, 14

What is your favorite place and why?

When we returned to California for the summer, we got to see a lot of family, catch up, and just hang out. It was fun staying at my grandparents' house and joining them for everyday things like going to the movies, the farmers' market, and my favorite stores, learning to play tennis, and biking. The simple stuff.

Was there any place you did not enjoy? Why?

Camping in Australia when we drove for what seemed forever on a windy road in the dark to get to Mossman's Tableland Caravan Park. It was in the middle of nowhere. We didn't get there until really late at night.

The place wasn't great. There were bugs like cockroaches and spiderwebs in the bathroom, and we had to walk pretty far in the dark to get there from our van. I even remembered a gecko. Luckily, we got there late and left early in the morning. Mommy wanted to get out of there quickly.

Where is home? What do you miss about it? Do you get homesick?

My home will always be in California, where my family is. That's where a lot of my childhood memories, like first riding a bike, playing the piano, going to preschool and kindergarten, and making friends all happened.

I remember our house. I always compare everything to that house. That's the standard.

Homesick? Not anymore. I used to get homesick because it was different not seeing family around and being in a new place.

We returned two summers ago, and the best part was having so much family close around. I miss that.

I see how cool it is to live abroad. I know we are eventually going back, so I'll enjoy the remaining time we have out here, wherever here is. I only have four to five years at most until I'll be back living in the US for college.

If you could live anywhere in the world, where would you?

Probably back in California, where we lived before, because all our family is there, and it's easier to make sense of the rules. There is no language barrier or anything.

Which place would you like to visit again?

I'd love to go back to Zehlendorf someday. It would be interesting to see how it has changed.

- The pathway that led to Heinrich Laehr Park. It was lined with small gardens that people would rent out and take care of really well.
- That one park by Edeka that had a climbing rock. My friend and I would chase each other, playing tag on it.
- Visit Edeka and get that granola cereal with the blue box.
- Go to Crispy's Chicken and get a döner kebab and pommes.

- Rathaus Steiglitz and go to Zur Bratpfanne. The burgers were almost as good as In-n-Out.

What has been your favorite experience?

That week it snowed in Berlin. We borrowed a sled from Mommy's friend, and I went out with my friends. Everyone in the neighborhood was going to the big hill by the school at Schönower Park. Most days, I would bike down it, but it was so much better sledding. It was super cold and fun. Normally, everything is brown and green. This was an exception when everything was coated in snow. It felt like Christmas, even though it was February. It was a new experience, and I could spend it with my friends.

What has been your worst experience?

The time when I was caught playing Minecraft at 3 a.m. and got grounded. That night was the worst because I had to sleep on the floor. I imagined cockroaches crawling over me.

For the next couple of weeks, I had to run two miles in the morning and then one mile in the afternoon. I was super tired.

What are the differences between your life abroad and back in California? How would you describe your lifestyle?

California revolved around family and events. You know, parties and stuff. Every weekend, there's someone's birthday or something. Things were also much more relaxed. In Germany or Hong Kong, is more about just us. We get to do a bunch of things. It's go-go-go—visit this place, eat at this restaurant, go on this hike, see this temple.

What do you think about your parents?

They are persistent. No matter the weather or how they were feeling, they were always getting the things we needed to do done.

For example, with Mommy and running. Even if she is sick or gets home late at night, she will wake up at 5 a.m. to get her seven miles in for the day. If there was a show to watch or a hike, Daddy would convince Mommy that we needed to do it. If I needed to run or get work finished, they made sure that I did it, even if I didn't want to.

What do you think about your parents' choice to leave the US and live abroad with you? If you had a choice, would you do it again? Why or why not?

I like to think of it in phases. Before we left, I really wanted to move because it sounded like it was going to be a cool trip. I remember I was so excited the whole time. I was a bit sad that I wasn't going to see my friends and family, but then I figured they would visit.

After a few months, once all the newness and surprises faded, life went from feeling special to normal. At that point, I wanted to go back.

And sometimes, when we were traveling, I didn't want to do all this work. All the packing, walking around, all the work that comes along with traveling. Biking ten miles and walking 100 miles to see a church or old house doesn't seem fun to me.

After our first year in Germany, something clicked, and I really started appreciating the experiences we were having. I'm not sure what it was or why, but it did.

Knowing what I know now, I'd do it again.

What do you think about the past five years?

Sometimes, I think not about what we are doing currently but what it's like when we go back.

How will I have changed?

I remember wondering about our return. Would I be seen as a hero, like in the movies, when the main character comes back from a battle? Will I be able to speak German? Will I be so different that people won't be able to recognize me?

I can't answer your question because I was eight or nine when we left. I was a different person. Now, I'm more independent, and I'm not sure if that's because of my surroundings or just because I'm older.

I'd be curious to compare myself to if I stayed. Would I have continued to play American football? Would I have different interests? Would I still be playing the piano instead of the guitar?

What advice can you give to a kid your age who is about to go live abroad for the first time?

I recommend keeping a journal or a log, documenting every week. It's a good way to keep track of time and how you have improved. Someday, it will be nostalgic to read.

I didn't do it myself, but I wish I did.

LEA LIGAYA, 12

What is your favorite place, and why?

France's Verdon Gorge. I liked it because we were with Elizabeth and her family.

We did some hiking, but we didn't do "hiking" hiking. We walked along the water and did a lot of swimming.

The water was a bright, pure aqua, and you couldn't see through it, which was a bit scary.

There was a bridge that had a sign that said no jumping because a lot of people died. People still jumped off. We also got to ride a boat through there, which was beautiful.

Where is home? What do you miss about it? Not miss? Do you get homesick?

Home is San Ramon because that is where I was born and that's where I lived the longest. California, seven years; Germany, two years; and Hong Kong, three years. If you asked me where I live right now, it's Hong Kong. Home right now is Hong Kong. Home in the whole wide world is California.

California has a lot better candy. There is no original Hong Kong candy. It seems as if everything is imported. They have Jolly Ranchers, Mike and Ikes, and all the good chocolates.

When we are there, you can buy jumbo packs. Ferrero Rocher chocolates only come in packs of four here. In the US, you can get the stuff at Costco in a pack of eight by six. For Mike and Ikes, the box only has 20 pieces. Back home, you can get a 1.8-pound bag for much cheaper.

The only good gum in Hong Kong is Wrigley's Doublemint. Back in the US, they have the Ice Breakers that come in cubes and all the flavors and actually tastes good. Back home, there were a lot more familiar brands. Here, it's a lot of random stuff.

Sometimes, it's too sunny in California. I have sunglasses, but I only like putting them on my head. I don't like wearing them. I hate being outside, and it's so bright that when I go inside, my vision is bluish-black. I don't like that adjustment.

I don't get homesick because this is home right now, which means I'm living at home, so how can I be homesick?

There were a few times I just wanted to go back home to our apartments in Berlin and Hong Kong.

When we were in Australia, we'd do, like, four hikes a day. Mommy says that some hikes didn't count because they were only one kilometer, but then others that were 15 kilometers. We would have to fold the bed every day. No devices the whole trip. All we had was music and the window view. Sometimes you need a bit of screen time. It's healthy for you.

When we are staying at a really bad hotel, I'd rather be at home. It was more comfortable and familiar at home. You can trust the stuff and know how things work, like the shower. You don't have to figure out how to turn it on or look for the water heater.

At home, we might have a couch that has a stain, but you know what caused that. If you go to a new place that has something dirty, you are left wondering how it got that way.

If you could live anywhere in the world, where would you?

I want to live in a cottage with wildflowers, a nearby beach, and a lake, and also a strawberry field, just like the one in Percy Jackson next to Camp Half-Blood.

I'd live in a vacation house but be there long term. Do you know what I mean? The type of house you'd stay in when you are on vacation. Instead of staying there just for vacation, I'd live there all the time.

I'd also want a job where I do hardly anything but get paid a lot for doing a little. I want food delivered to my house. I want my friends to live next to me.

What has been your favorite experience?

Mountain climbing in Iceland. We just arrived in Iceland and spent the first few days in quarantine. We had a nice Airbnb with a hot tub, and during the day, it was okay to walk around because it was far from everything, and nobody was around. It was snowing, and everything was white.

There was no trail, and we decided to go up the nearby mountain. It's not like Hong Kong, where there is a trail that you follow and do it for exercise. When you are climbing a mountain, it's fun because you have to think on your own. It's out in the open. You are constantly choosing where to go and have lots of options. I like that kind of environment.

The best part was when it started to get steep toward the tippie top. My parents were too scared to go any further. "You can't go to close to the edge, or you'll cause an avalanche." To get down, we slid on the side of the mountain. We were going so fast. Do you remember in Frozen 2 when Elsa was sliding through the cave? It was like that.

I'd like to visit Austria again. We didn't have to do any exercise. It was a relaxing holiday, and we spent a lot of time playing in the snow. I remember getting hit by a snowball, and I started bleeding. We did some sledding. While exploring, we found a large patch of ice, and we made it our open ice rink. The whole experience had a nice vibe.

Iceland was tiring. We were constantly packing up our stuff, and there was a lot to do every day. We were so busy going from one place to the next.

Which place would you like to visit again?

Hvar, Croatia. It was chill, but we also did a lot of stuff. Lots of island hopping. I even remember getting a yummy dessert with a waffle cone with layers of Nutella. It was even better because Feris couldn't have any because it had nuts, so that meant more for Jero and me.

The place we stayed was really nice. Jero was in a cooking phase, and he wanted to help in the kitchen all the time. There were two floors and a huge pink bougainvillea plant that covered the front. Every meal, we would get gelato. There were a lot of beaches to visit and places to play in the sand.

If not Hvar, Greece would be another option because it was similar.

What has been your worst experience?

I don't know. Maybe it's a really bad hotel or something, but I can't think of one because I'm a positive person.

The Iceland hike where we went to the volcano. It wasn't the worst, but it was a bad experience.

Everyone wanted to see the erupting volcano, so we walked in a herd of people like we were in a Disneyland line. There was mud everywhere, and it got on my shoes, pants, and hands. Luckily, I didn't fall. It was really cold, and it smelled of sulfur.

Once we got there, it was great, seeing the volcano up close erupting and the lava flowing. It was just the hike to get there that was not fun.

The worst was camping in Sai Kung with my school class. Everything was fun except for the bathrooms. There was only one actual toilet, and the counselors kept it for themselves.

All the kids had to use the squat toilets. They were nasty. People would pee and miss, so it would be everywhere. There was even poo that was the size of a buffalo that didn't go in the hole, so it just sat there and made the bathroom smell. It was so unhygienic.

The showers had cockroaches. There was only cold water, and it came down as a trickle. Hardly anything came out. We were timed, and people were always rushing. Girls would come out with shampoo still in their hair. I bet the counselor showers were better. And because we had to wear shoes at the campground, we had to put on our socks right after the shower. That meant that I had wet socks.

And it was freezing cold, the coldest I've ever been in Hong Kong. It was Iceland cold for three days.

What are the differences between your life abroad and back in California? How would you describe your lifestyle?

California is a lot more chill. Don't need to do as much as stuff. I mean, there is less to do.

To go anywhere is a long commute. All you do is live there. You don't feel like you are in a rush to do anything.

Here, you can take the ferry, bus, or train. It can take you anywhere you want to go. It's super easy.

Can't buy things for the long term, like a motorized scooter because you might need to sell it.

Can't get good furniture. You need to buy IKEA stuff or used because you'll need to get rid of it when you move.

What do you think about your parents?

All my friends say you are super young, and I talk to you like business partners. My friends talk to their parents like parents.

My parents pretend they don't want me to do bad things, but they want me to do bad things. I vandalized a house and trespassed into an abandoned building, and they were okay with it.

They don't tell you not to do things. They tell you to do things, and if you don't, you get a consequence.

What do you think about your parents' choice to leave the US and live abroad with you? If you had a choice, would you do it again? Why or why not?

It's a good idea because we wouldn't be doing anything if we just stayed in California. It's all the same people. If you had bad blood with someone, you would be stuck with them. It's a small town, and no one is moving.

Living in Hong Kong will make for a good college essay someday.

Also, all my best friends are here so I wouldn't have met them if we hadn't moved.

What do you think about the past five years?

We walked a lot and saw a lot of stuff. I probably have seen more than people three times my age. Most people don't travel.

It's very repetitive. We wake up early, get to a place, and check into a hotel that is either good or bad. Walk somewhere and get food and then we have to walk further because we have to find the food. After we eat, we walk somewhere to check something out. We go back to the hotel and then head out again so that we can walk again. Repeat until it's time to go home, and we catch a flight. We will get back late, unpack our bags, and sleep late.

What advice can you give to a kid your age who is about to go live abroad for the first time?

You need a good wardrobe, attire, and gear, or else you'll get uncomfortable. For example, you can't have a wheelie backpack at our school because there are a lot of stairs. It doesn't work. You can't dress touristy, or people will know, and they will treat you like a tourist, especially those people trying to make money. They will talk to you and raise their prices.

Life isn't that different. It's easy to adjust to. It's just a different place. You'll probably go to an international school where you can speak your language, and it makes it a lot easier.

The only thing to worry about and prepare for is that your parents will probably make you walk a lot to see random things.

FERIS MALAYA, 9

What is your favorite place, and why?

Iceland because we saw a volcano and stayed at a cabin with video games and a hot tub. We had pizza for several nights. We also went up mountains and swam in a hot spring.

Was there any place you did not enjoy? Why?

We got to Hanoi, Vietnam, really late. The hotel we stayed at separated us into two different small rooms. I was grumpy because I was tired and hungry. There weren't enough towels, and the shower wasn't good. The water didn't get hot enough, and it would make a mess all over the floor. Luckily, we only stayed a few hours because we got there late and left early in the morning.

I liked Hanoi, but not that hotel. I would give it a three out of ten.

Where is home? What do you miss about it? Not miss? Do you get homesick?

The US. I miss going to Target or Mama Becky and Papa Joker's house because they have a lot of plants, fruits, and pineapple sausages. I remember when we went crabbing. We caught one, but Lea killed it. Neighborhood parties. I don't get homesick because there are a lot of fun things here, just like in the US.

What has been your favorite experience?

Iceland.

When we returned to the cabin from a walk, I remember that you threw us into really deep snow.

I also liked the hot spring. There was algae at the bottom, and there were other people there. When we had to get out, it was freezing cold.

There was also a hot tub in the middle of nowhere. When we stuck our heads out, it was so cold that ice would form.

These were fun things, and we did a lot of exploring.

I'd like to visit Greece again because we stayed at a place, where they made food for us. It was really good. There were pool floaties, and we went to the beaches. I forgot the rest.

I also liked France because we went to the lavender fields. It was really pretty. I didn't like the bees.

We stayed in a really big house with the Steeles. I don't remember where that was, but I know it was in France.

In Croatia, we rode in a speedboat, and Lea and I sat in the front. The wind felt nice, but we had to wear a life vest. The water was cold. They warned us if a sea urchin stung us, we would have to pee on the sting.

Which place would you like to visit again?

Iceland because of all the things I shared earlier.

What has been your worst experience?

That hotel in Hanoi was on the list.

I have to walk upstairs every day at school and when heading home. It's really hilly here.

If you could live anywhere in the world, where would you?

Hawai'i because there were lots of water activities. When we went a few summers ago, we played in the water every day. We also got to play with a dog named Soju and take care of him.

What are the differences between your life abroad and back in California? How would you describe your lifestyle?

We get to travel a lot, and I make more friends easily because we have more in common. In the US, I only did a few activities, but when we travel, we get to do a lot of stuff, and I share those in common with the people I meet at school.

Here, I wake up and do my routine. I then walk to school instead of being driven. My school isn't far away.

What do you think about your parents?

In Japan, when we were heading back to our hotel in Osaka, we thought we were on the right train. We then got to our seats, and someone was sitting in them. We talked to the train conductor, who explained we were on the wrong train heading in the opposite direction. We had to wait an hour till the next stop. We always get lost, but we find our way back.

My parents are good people.

What do you think about your parents' choice to leave the US and live abroad with you? If you had a choice, would you do it again? Why or why not?

It's a good choice because we get to travel, have explored so many new places, and tried new foods like phở, udon, kimchi fried rice, kimbap, mango sticky rice, new boba places, and Bun Cha.

What do you think about the past five years?

I don't know.

What advice can you give to a kid your age who is about to go live abroad for the first time?

You shouldn't care too much about your toys, objects, or thingamajigs because you'll probably have to let it go. There won't be a lot of space if you are going to move somewhere different, and it's hard to carry all that stuff.

Say goodbye to your friends early, if not, it might turn into a quick goodbye, or you won't be able to say goodbye at all.

Made in United States
North Haven, CT
24 April 2024

51682122R10214